BRITISH AIRPORTS

THEN & NOW

The prototype de Havilland DH95 Flamingo parked in front of the terminal and control tower at Jersey Airport in May 1939 whilst on loan to Guernsey and Jersey Airlines. *Quadrant Picture Library*

BRITISH AIRPORTS

THEN & NOW

LEO MARRIOTT

IAN ALLAN Publishing

Previous page:
A busy scene on the ramp at Cardiff Wales Airport during the summer of 1992 when adverse weather across the Severn estuary had caused several aircraft to divert from Bristol Airport. *Malcolm Bradbury*

Published by Ian Allan Ltd, Shepperton, Surrey; and printed in Great Britain by Ian Allan Printing Ltd, Coombelands House, Addlestone, Surrey KT15 1HY

First published 1993

ISBN 0 7110 2076 0

CONTENTS

BIBLIOGRAPHY AND ACKNOWLEDGEMENTS 6

GLOSSARY 6

INTRODUCTION 7

1. LONDON'S AIRPORTS 13

2. BIRMINGHAM, WALES AND THE MIDLANDS 49

3. MANCHESTER AND THE NORTH 67

4. SOUTH AND WEST 93

5. SCOTLAND AND NORTHERN IRELAND 121

6. GOVERNMENT AND INDUSTRY 139

APPENDICES:

I. AIRPORT IDENTIFICATION CODES 155

II. PASSENGER STATISTICS 158

Glossary

ATC	Air Traffic Control
ATCC	Air Traffic Control Centre
BAA	British Airports Authority
BEA	British European Airways
BOAC	British Overseas Airways Corporation
BoT	Board of Trade
CAA	Civil Aviation Authority
D/F	Direction Finding (Radio)
DoTi	Department of Trade and Industry
ERTS	Elementary and Reserve Training School
EFTS	Elementary Flying Training School
FAA	Fleet Air Arm
ILS	Instrument Landing System
IRVR	Instrumented Runway Visual Range
IT	Inclusive Tour
MTCA	Ministry of Transport and Civil Aviation
MoA	Ministry of Aviation
NEC	National Exhibition Centre (Birmingham)
OTU	Operational Training Unit
RAF	Royal Air Force
RAFVR	Royal Air Force Volunteer Reserve
RAuxAF	Royal Auxiliary Air Force
RFC	Royal Flying Corps
RFS	Refresher Flying School
R/W	Runway
SBAC	Society of British Aerospace Companies
UAS	University Air Squadron
USAAF	United States Army Air Force
VDF	VHF Direction Finding
VDU	Visual Display Unit
VTOL	Vertical Take-Off and Landing
VHF	Very High Frequency

Bibliography and Acknowledgements

Although much of the information contained in this book was provided by the management and public relations staff at many of the airfields described, extensive reference was also made to various published sources and the author gratefully acknowledges the detailed research already carried out by the writers and historians concerned. Apart from numerous magazines, brochures and handbooks, the following publications were of particular value.

Action Stations (9 Vols).
   Various authors. Published by Patrick Stephens Ltd. 1981-85
Airports of the World.
   John Stroud. Putnam. 1980
Bottlang Airfield Manual
   Jeppesen Sanderson Inc. 1992
British Airports
   J.W.R.Taylor. Ian Allan Ltd. 1964
British Airports.
   Alan J.Wright. Ian Allan Ltd. Various editions to 1988
Britain's Military Airfields 1939-45
   David J.Smith. Patrick Stephens Ltd. 1989
British Independent Airlines since 1946 (4 Vols)
   A.C.Merton Jones. LAAS International/Merseyside Aviation Soc. 1976
Major Airports of the World.
   Roy Allen. Ian Allan Ltd. 1979/1983
Military Airfields in the British Isles 1939-45.
   S.Willis and B.Holliss. Enthusiasts Publications. 1987.

The airfield plans used in this book come from two sources. Those showing prewar airfields are taken from the 1935 edition of the Air Pilot published by the Air Ministry as a guide to pilots flying within British airspace. Plans showing the current layout of airports are taken from the latest edition of the Air Pilot and are published by kind permission of the Civil Aviation Authority.

Introduction

It is a sobering thought that, around the world, over 1,000 billion passengers are boarding scheduled airline flights every year and the figure is constantly increasing. Added to this are millions of charter passengers as well as others on private or business flights and all of these have one thing in common — they will begin and end their flight at an airport. Those with an interest in aviation affairs will inevitably concentrate their attention on the aircraft themselves, perhaps the most exciting machines ever invented by man, but from the very earliest days aviators have always been dependent on support from the ground. Of course, their original demands were few, any reasonably flat area would do for taking-off and landing and a few gallons of fuel could be easily carried in cans. However, early aircraft were fragile and at the mercy of the elements and so some sort of weatherproof shelter soon became a necessity. As aircraft got larger and heavier, they needed longer take-off and landing runs and so aerodromes became larger, although still very small by modern standards.

While such simple facilities sufficed for pilots and their aircraft, the introduction of commercial passenger flying after World War 1 meant that better accommodation was required and the start of international flights, mainly between France and Britain, meant that HM Customs and Excise became involved and the idea of an Air Port was born. However, passenger numbers were still very small, many so-called airliners were single-engined biplanes carrying only two or three passengers, and it was not until around 1930 that air travel became safe and comfortable enough to begin attracting a worthwhile market. Aircraft such as the de Havilland Dragon, Westland Wessex and Spartan Cruiser had operating economics which enabled the first comprehensive network of domestic air services to be established while stately, if uninspired, multi-engined biplanes such as the Handley Page HP42 took care of long-range flights to Europe and further afield. All of these aircraft could fly quite happily from grass airfields as take-off and landing speeds were low, and even the HP42 weighed in at less than 30,000lb — considerably lighter than one of today's fully loaded commuter aircraft such as a Dash 8.

The 1930s saw a boom in the opening of British airports, most of them owned by city corporations keen to see their towns firmly established on the aeronautical map. Indeed there seems to have been considerably more air mindedness amongst the various town hall officials than there ever is today when the mere idea of a new airport is the signal for well orchestrated opposition groups to swing into action. Most of the airfields set up in the 1930s consisted only of a relatively flat grass area, a small administration building and a hangar or two. However, by 1939 many had grown significantly and some, such as Croydon, Heston, Liverpool, Jersey, Manchester and Glasgow, had invested in imposing buildings, the latest navigation aids and flying control facilities. Aircraft had increased in size, weight and complexity, and it was becoming apparent that simple grass airfields, no matter how large, would not support intensive use by new types of aircraft, such as the de Havilland Albatross and Flamingo, the Armstrong Whitworth Ensign, and most importantly, the new breed of high speed monoplanes from America epitomised by the DC-3 and its projected successors.

The question of providing paved runways was already being considered prior to the outbreak of war and they were already common in the United States. Manchester's Barton airport laid claim to being the first in the UK with American-style runways although in fact these consisted only of a rolled cinder bed, an expedient forced on the airport's owners by the soggy nature of the surface. The only civil hard runway in the country in 1939 appears to have been at Bristol's Whitchurch Down and for that reason was selected as Imperial Airways' base on the outbreak of war. The first RAF station to have a runway was Cranwell where one was laid in 1928 as part of a programme for experimental long-range flights but, by 1939, only a handful of other airfields were so equipped. However, by 1942 the Air Force had settled into a policy of laying 2,000yd runways with two subsidiary shorter runways at almost all of its operational fields. When the American Air Force arrived, they joined in the airfield construction programme with vigour and, by 1945, the country was covered with modern airfields capable of operating the latest aircraft.

Many of these airfields had previously been civil airports and were requisitioned in 1939 but, with the coming of peace, the government was slow to return them to their previous owners. Instead their operation and development came under the control of the Ministry of Civil Aviation (later to pass through many guises as the MTCA, MoA, BoT, DoTi, and finally CAA). This reflected a postwar policy of state control of the air transport industry in the same way that the railways were nationalised in 1948. In the air, the state-owned BEA ran air services to the various state-owned airports around the country. In addition, the government funded the enormous expense of developing Heathrow as Britain's major international airport, later to be followed by Gatwick in the mid-1950s. Although some airfields, such as Southend, were returned to private or municipal ownership from 1947 onwards, it was not until around 1960 that the government began seriously divesting itself of other airports such as Liverpool (1961), Southampton (1961), and Blackbushe (1960).

Birmingham was one of many municipal airports opened during the late 1930s and its distinctive prewar terminal building remained in use until superseded by the new terminal complex on the other side of the airfield in 1984. The photograph shows a Viscount of BEA during the 1960s.
Birmingham International Airport

In the meantime technical improvements in aircraft were forcing airport authorities to provide better facilities such as longer runways, larger terminals, radar, runway and approach lighting, and instrument landing systems. After the postwar generation of piston-engined airliners came the first turboprops, notably the Viscount Herald and Friendship, and these generally required around 1,600m of runway. By the end of the 1950s the jet revolution was underway, initially at the major airports such as Heathrow, but by the mid-1960s aircraft such as the BAC-111 and Trident were being used on domestic services and these demanded at least a 2,000m runway. Intercontinental jets required up to 3,000, and today Heathrow, Gatwick, Stansted and Manchester can offer runways in excess of that figure. In fact Heathrow's longest runway is almost 4,000m. However, despite the ever increasing size of modern airliners, advances in engine technology and aerodynamics mean that runway length is less critical than it used to be and many regional airports now regularly dispatch transatlantic charter flights from runways with a typical length of 2,500m or less.

The advent of wide-bodied jets in the early 1970s initially caused major problems at airports where terminal buildings, baggage handling facilities and Customs and Immigration procedures suddenly had to deal with passengers arriving and departing in packages of 400 to 500 at a time. At the same time the physical size and weight of these aircraft meant that runways and taxiways had to be strengthened, parking bays enlarged and fire and rescue facilities increased. By the end of the decade the major airports had been rebuilt to meet these requirements and the boom in IT charters meant that the regional airports also began to receive wide-bodied aircraft and had to be upgraded accordingly. Much of the money for these programmes has come from EEC funds, a point perhaps not appreciated by the average holiday traveller who takes it for granted that he can fly to Florida and other exotic parts of the world from his local airport.

Another factor which has had an effect on the layout and running of all airports is the sickening rise in terrorist attacks on aviation-related targets. Following some dramatic hijacks in the 1980s, security is a top priority (and legal requirement) at any airport operating scheduled services. The installation of expensive and sophisticated search and detection devices, together with the employment of a small army of security staff, is now an unwelcome burden on the finances of the airports concerned. In many cases this has also led to the closure of spectator terraces and other parts of the airfield to members of the public, while extensive security fencing ensures that no unauthorised person can get anywhere near the aircraft. While these measures are obviously necessary, they have had the effect of making airports less accessible and, indeed, it is possible to visit some without being able to see an aircraft at all. There are some exceptions, such as Manchester and East Midlands, where positive efforts have been made to provide viewing facilities, well away from the main terminal areas, from where the young enthusiast, perhaps tomorrow's pilot, air traffic controller or airport manager, can pursue his hobby.

This book attempts, through the medium of photographs, to show some of the history of our airports and how they have grown and developed over the years. While all the major airports have been covered in varying detail, an effort has been made to include a large cross-section of the many smaller or less busy airfields which, nevertheless, play an important part in the communities they serve. Space does not permit the inclusion of every airfield and there are bound to be some omissions,

Oxford Airport has traditionally been a base for flying training since it opened in 1938 and, in terms of aircraft movements, it is probably one of the busiest airfields in the UK. The Oxford Air Training School, one of whose aircraft is shown standing in front of the modern control tower, trains pilots and engineers from all over the world. *Author*

mainly of those places where it has proved difficult to obtain suitable photos. The interpretation of the term 'airport' has been in its most general sense in order to include some civil airfields which, although rich in history, are not actually involved in commercial passenger flying. In addition, several airports which have played their part in the development of British aviation but which have now closed down are also included. As far as possible aerial photographs have been used as these best show the airfield layout and are useful for comparative purposes. Most of these photographs have come from the excellent and extensive collection built up over the years by Aerofilms and, for the convenience of any reader wishing to order copies, the reference number is given in each case.

Finally, the reader will come across many references to runways and their designators, and it may be appropriate to explain how these are derived for the benefit of those not familiar with the system. Basically a runway is designated according to the direction of the axis of its centreline with respect to magnetic north and the resulting figure is rounded up or down to the nearest tens to give a two figure number. Thus a runway with a QDR (a prewar morse code group meaning magnetic bearing, but still used as a current abbreviation) of 281° would be designated Runway 28, while another with a QDR of 136° would become Runway 14. Of course, the axis of a runway can be measured in two directions, each 180° out from the other. Thus a runway which was exactly aligned on an east-west axis (with respect to magnetic north) would have QDRs 090°/270° and would be known as 09/27. A few airports have two runways running parallel to each other and in this case the letters L and R are added to indicate Left or Right although the only example in the UK is Heathrow which has 09L/27R and 09R/27L (Gatwick also has parallel runways but one of these is normally used as a taxiway, having been strengthened for use as a standby runway if the main runway is closed for any reason). Because the magnetic north pole moves, the runway QDR will slowly alter over a period of years which occasionally leads to a runway designator being changed. Heathrow again provides an example as its main runways changed from 10/28 to 09/27 a few years ago when the QDR fell from 276° to 275°. However, as the magnetic variation changes only by around 10 minutes of arc each year, it will be at least 60 years before another change is required.

Mention of runways prompts an explanation of some of the white runway markings which will be noted when looking at the aerial photos of various airports. For a pilot coming in to land the nearest symbols will normally be the row of parallel bars, otherwise known as the 'piano keys', which indicate the start of the runway proper and is called the threshold. On no account should he attempt to touch down before crossing the threshold, even though there may be a stretch of tarmac available. At some airfields one or more white crosses may precede the threshold markings and these indicate that that particular section of the runway is permanently closed and should not be used. This is often the case at old wartime airfields which have been reopened and only a section of the original runway is suitable for use. Another variation is a line of arrows pointing along the axis of the runway before the threshold and these indicate that the first section of the runway may be used as part of the take-off run, but landings should be made further down the runway, past the threshold. Once over the threshold, the pilot will see the figures of the runway designator and a dashed centreline, similar to ordinary road markings. Additionally he will see single long white bars near the side of the runway and these mark the 500, 1500 and 2000 ft points from the threshold, while a group of three such bars on each side of the runway mark the 1,000ft point. These markings delineate the touchdown zone but are found only on runways which are served by a precision approach aid, such as ILS.

It would be possible to write a whole book on the technical features of airports which might be seen in the photographs which illustrate this book. However, this is not intended as a technical manual, merely a general and, hopefully, interesting overview of the many airports which serve the towns and cities of Britain. At the end of this book an appendix gives details of the numbers of passengers using each airport over the years since 1958, but for a brief overview of the dramatic way in which air travel has become part of our everyday lives the following table provides some interesting data.

Leo Marriott
December 1992

Photographic Note: Almost half of the illustrations in this book are aerial photograpahs from the archives of Aerofilms. Readers wishing to obtain copies of these may order them directly from the company quoting the negative number given alongside each photo. Aerofilms have generously offered a 25% discount from their standard rates on orders of pictures from this book. Write to: Aerofilms Ltd, Gate Studios, Borehamwood, Herts WD6 1EJ.

Copies of photos credited to the Quadrant Picture Library (QPL) are obtainable from them at Quadrant House, The Quadrant, Sutton, Surrey SM2 5AS.

Combined statistics for UK airfields 1951-1990

Year	Total Movements (x1,000)	Total passengers (x1,000)
1951	499	2,471
1960	754	10,075
1970	1,468	31,606
1980	2,181	57,823
1990	3,255	102,418

These figures, and other statistics quoted in this book, are taken from the comprehensive annual statements of UK Airport data published by the Civil Aviation Authority.

1.
London's
Airports

Heathrow: A dramatic wide angle view of Heathrow's Runway 27L during a typical busy period. In the foreground a queue of seven aircraft wait their turn for take-off clearance. A DC-9 is half way down the runway while a British Airways 747 waits in the distance to cross from the Terminal 4 apron. In the background on the left is the World Cargo Centre which handles over 700,000 tons of air freight a year, no less than 75% of the total passing through all UK airports. The relentless increase in passenger traffic, only briefly checked in the aftermath of the Gulf War, continues to put pressure on existing facilities and Terminal 4 has already been extended since it opened. The next expansion will be a Terminal 5, which will be built, subject to planning approval, on the Perry Oaks site at the west end of the airfield, and will be able to cope with the projected 600-800 seater airliners now being designed by Airbus, Boeing and McDonnell Douglas. Phase 1 is expected to open in 2002 and when finally complete, in 2016, Terminal 5 will boost Heathrow's capacity to around 80 million passengers a year. *Aerofilms 595901*

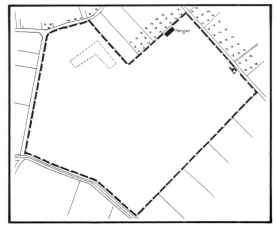

Above:

Heathrow: London's Heathrow is Britain's premier airport and one of the busiest in the world. At peak times over 12,000 passengers an *hour* pass through its four terminals and there are well over 1,000 aircraft movements a day, almost all being large passenger jets. It is therefore difficult to imagine Heathrow as it was in the 1930s, a small private grass airfield rejoicing in the title of 'Great West Aerodrome'. Owned by the Fairey Company, it was used mainly for test flying and most commercial flights operated from nearby Heston or Hanworth Park. The diagrams show the position and layout of the airfield in 1935, the minimal facilities consisting only of a single hangar. Like most other contemporary airfields it was requisitioned by the Air Ministry, although not until 1944 when the site was earmarked for development as a major transport base with paved runways to supplement and eventually replace Northolt. The original plan called for the standard RAF triangular pattern of three runways but the war ended before work was completed.

Right:

Heathrow: With the coming of peace in 1945 it was evident that commercial aviation would have an increasingly important role in the development of postwar Britain. Wartime technical developments had brought about startling changes in the capacity and performance of airliners and it was obvious that London required a large modern airport equipped with long runways, modern navigation aids, engineering facilities and passenger terminals. The partly built site at Heathrow was an obvious starting point and it was therefore handed over to the Ministry of Civil Aviation on 1 January 1946. By this time the first runway had been completed and rudimentary passenger facilities were in place, in tents, adjacent to the Bath Road on the north side of the airfield. The three original runways were completed by 1947 and work continued on a further three which were intended to provide a pair of parallel runways in each of three directions, the overall plan resembling the six pointed Star of David (a scaling down of one design which proposed no less than nine runways!). In 1950 work began on terminal facilities in the central area while, at the same time, BEA and BOAC started to establish their engineering facilities and hangars on the east side of the airfield. This 1954 photo shows the BEA hangar shortly after completion with Viscounts and Elizabethans parked in the foreground. In the background work progresses on the BOAC hangar and between the two buildings are a number of laid up aircraft including several Vikings and three Hermes. In the right background is the Hatton Cross roundabout adjacent to the A30 trunk road. This is now the site of one of Heathrow's three Underground stations. *Aerofilms A54488*

Below right:

Heathrow: The central area at Heathrow pictured in 1957. The new terminal facilities had been formally opened by HM The Queen in 1955 and consisted of the combined Britannic and Europa buildings in the foreground which now form the basis of today's Terminal 2, and the Queen's Building on the right which housed airline and airport administrative offices. The substantial control tower, in the centre, remains largely unaltered today. The development of the central area cut across the line of what would have been Runway 15R/33L but by this time the concept of six runways had been abandoned as unnecessary and already other buildings were springing up on the concrete section then completed. Visible in the top right corner of the central area is the entrance to the tunnel which provided the link to the outside world. This seemed a forward thinking idea at the time, but today it imposes a severe constraint on access to the terminals due to the unforeseen volume of modern traffic. *Aerofilms A69785*

Right:
Heathrow: Heathrow's central area initially only catered for domestic and near European services, long range intercontinental traffic continuing to use the north side. Although the tents had long since been replaced when this photo was taken in 1960, the 'terminal' consisted in the main of a series of interconnecting huts and temporary structures. Although less than two years since the introduction of jets on the north Atlantic routes, the extent of the revolution wrought can be seen by looking at the line up of aircraft on the apron which, apart from a KLM DC-6B and DC-3, are all jets and turboprops. In the background are three Boeing 707s belonging to Pan American, TWA and Air India while in the foreground are several BOAC Comet 4s and Britannias, plus an El Al Britannia (second from the right).
Aerofilms A81851

Left:
Heathrow: Also taken in 1960, this view of the central area shows work underway on the new 'Oceanic' terminal, later to become Terminal 3, which eventually opened at the end of 1961 for use by BOAC with other long haul carriers moving in the following year. In the background new aircraft parking areas have been added, further encroaching on areas of concrete laid down as runways in the original plan. Aircraft in this picture provide a snapshot of the period with Viscounts, Elizabethans and Comet 4Bs much in evidence while the row in the foreground includes two Caravelles, a Tu-104 and a Lockheed L1049G Super Constellation. The continuing mix of piston and jet engined types made this one of Heathrow's most interesting periods for the aviation enthusiast.
Aerofilms A81852

Above:
Heathrow: A bird's eye view of Heathrow in 1986. Development of the central area is complete with Terminal 1 (opened in 1968) in the northeast corner, Terminal 2 in the southeast corner and Terminal 3 on the western side, and all three are served by an extensive network of piers and holding lounges. However, increasing congestion in the central area led to the construction of the all-new Terminal 4 which opened in 1986 and now handles over 8 million passengers a year out of the airport's total of 42 million in 1990. Today there are only three runways in use, the east-west 09L/27R and 09R/27L with lengths of 3,902m and 3,658m respectively (upper and lower in the picture), and the shorter 05/23 which is 2,357m long (top right to bottom left). On the right is the distinctive square shape of the new British Airways hangar which adjoins the old BEA hangar shown in the earlier photograph. The north side of the airfield has now been completely abandoned by aircraft; the former taxiway is now a staff and long term car park.
Aerofilms A505750

Left:
Heathrow: Inside the Control Tower at Heathrow during 1963. On the right is the Ground Movement Controller (GMC) and his assistants. When an aircraft called for start-up the controller in the centre would contact the Southern Air Traffic Control Centre, then situated on the north side of the airfield, to request a clearance. He would write this on the Flight Progress strip and pass it to the GMC on his right who would direct the aircraft along the various taxiways to the holding point of the runway in use. Control of the aircraft would then pass to the Runway Controller, sitting with his assistant on the left of this picture, who would eventually clear it for take-off. Inbound aircraft were looked after by the radar-equipped Approach Control located beneath the VCR. They would pass inbound aircraft to the Runway Controller once they were established on final approach to land. *CAA via Quadrant Picture Library*

Left:
Heathrow: The Precision Approach Radar (PAR) at Heathrow in 1963. PAR was a very accurate radar which enabled the controller to monitor the progress of an aircraft on final approach in both azimuth and elevation. In the course of a talkdown he would pass heading and descent rate instructions to the pilot in order to ensure that the aircraft remained on the centreline and on the glidepath. The equipment mounted on stalks above the twin displays were small projectors which threw an accurate graticule representing the centreline and glidepath on to the radar screen. PAR was very labour intensive as the controller could only talkdown one aircraft at a time but by 1963 it was used mainly as a back-up for the ILS which was the standard approach aid and it was completely withdrawn in the early 1970s. *CAA via Quadrant Picture Library*

Below left:
Heathrow: The modern ATC set-up in the tower at Heathrow. In 1963 the airport handled just under 170,000 aircraft movements and this has increased to around 400,000 in 1992. Despite this, the control tower VCR has not been enlarged, although it has been updated from time to time. Compared to the 1963 layout, the most obvious addition is the high resolution surface radar and the use of VDUs to display information. Departing and arriving aircraft are subject to constant flow control by means of departure and arrival slots. Outbound aircraft fly specific Standard Instrument Departures (SIDs) which obviate the need to obtain specific clearances for each aircraft from the London ATCC (which is now at West Drayton a few miles north of the airfield). The Approach Control has been enlarged but this is due to be replaced in the near future by the CCF (Centralised Control Function) which will provide a combined approach service for all the major London airfields. The ATCC itself is due to move, to a new site near Southampton, in 1996. *CAA*

Gatwick: Currently handling around 20 million passengers a year, Gatwick is Britain's second busiest airport and has a history going back to 1931 when it was opened as a private airfield by Home Counties Aircraft Services. Subsequently it was developed by Airports Ltd who built the distinctive 'Beehive' terminal, with associated aprons and taxiways, which was opened in 1936. The adjacent Southern Railway station was reached by means of a subway and covered walkways were provided for access to aircraft. For the period it was an exceptionally forward-looking project which deserved more success than it achieved. The take-off and landing area, to the north of the terminal, was still grass surfaced and very prone to waterlogging so that British Airways, a forerunner of BEA, moved out to Heston and Croydon by 1938. During World War 2 the airfield was taken over by the RAF and extended to include the racecourse just visible in the background of the photo. By 1945 Gatwick was being used as a terminal for various communication squadrons flying between the UK and Europe — a foretaste of its eventual role. *Aerofilms C13612*

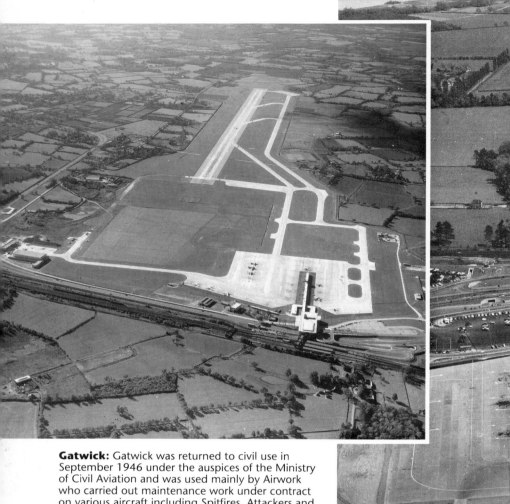

Gatwick: Gatwick was returned to civil use in September 1946 under the auspices of the Ministry of Civil Aviation and was used mainly by Airwork who carried out maintenance work under contract on various aircraft including Spitfires, Attackers and Sea Hornets. A few charter companies also took up residence but operations were limited due to the lack of paved runways. A significant user was the experimental BEA Helicopter Unit which used the old Beehive as its headquarters. In 1953 a government report nominated Gatwick as the site of London's second airport. The report was a model of brevity, only six pages long, and one can only imagine the tons of documents and public inquiries which would be mounted if such a decision were to be made today! The old airfield subsequently closed in 1956 to allow construction of a 2,000m main runway with a complex of connecting taxiways, and a new terminal incorporating a railway station. The new development was some distance to the northwest of the old Beehive which remained, although the railway was realigned to serve the new station. The photo was taken in 1959, a year after the airport officially reopened, and clearly shows the covered pier leading from the terminal to the aircraft parking stands — the first example in the UK of this now common feature of airport architecture.
Aerofilms A79262

Gatwick: As traffic increased in the 1960s the terminal was extended and two additional piers were constructed, as envisaged in the original plans. By 1964, when this photo was taken, work on the terminal extension, to the right of the central pier, is almost complete and a second pier, on the left, has been opened. Work is just commencing on a third pier and its projected outline can be seen. By this time Gatwick was handling around 1.1 million passengers a year and was in fact only Britain's fourth busiest airport behind Heathrow, Manchester and Glasgow. Traffic was mainly charter although British United Airways, the airport's main operator, was gradually building up a network of scheduled services. Among the few aircraft on the apron is an Ambassador belonging to Dan Air who, until their demise in 1992, were to become Gatwick's largest operator. *Aerofilms A128095.*

Gatwick: In the 1970s Gatwick saw a considerable expansion and began to come into its own as Britain's second airport. Further extensions were made to the terminal and substantial lounges were added to the central pier. The main runway was lengthened in stages to its present 3,159m and today the parallel taxiway has been widened and strengthened so that it can be used as an emergency runway. Aircraft parking aprons were considerably enlarged and surface communications have been improved with the opening of the M23 and M25 motorways. In 1978 Gatwick became a trans-Atlantic gateway as Braniff and Delta began scheduled services, in addition to those already being flown by British Caledonian, successor to British United. By 1980 almost 10 million passengers were using Gatwick each year and, like Heathrow, the increase was met by building additional terminals. The first of these was the circular satellite terminal which opened in 1982 and whose construction required the removal of the previous north pier. However, passenger figures doubled again during the 1980s and further capacity was provided by the construction of the entirely separate North Terminal which opened in 1988 and both of these developments are served by driverless rapid transit systems. On the apron in this 1988 view are aircraft of Nationair (Canada), Philippine Airlines, Continental, Delta, Wardair and Cathay Pacific — all reflecting Gatwick's status as a major international airport. *Aerofilms 537328*

22

Stansted: Stansted is now firmly established as London's third airport but reaching that status has been fraught with difficulty. The airfield was originally constructed by the USAAF in 1942/43 and was mainly used as a depot and maintenance unit although the 344th Bombardment Group was based here from May to September 1944. After the war there was some sporadic civilian use but the Ministry of Civil Aviation did not take over the airfield until 1949. During the Korean War the USAF moved in again and lengthened the runway to its present 3,000m — at that time one of the longest in the UK — but the Americans left in 1957 and civil operations continued on a relatively small scale. In 1958, for example, only 20,000 passengers were carried — even less than several small airfields such as Land's End and Kirkwall which both recorded in excess of 25,000 that year. However, the airfield provided a base for several non-passenger orientated activities such as the Ministry of Aviation Flying Unit Airwork, and Aviation Traders who concentrated their Carvair production here in 1961. At the time this photo was taken in 1966, passenger throughput had fallen to less than 10,000 a year but thereafter it began to rise steadily following the expansion of Channel Airways and the construction of a modest terminal building in the late 1960s which was sited adjacent to the hardstandings behind the control tower. *Aerofilms A160062*

Above:

Stansted: During the 1960s and 1970s Stansted began to develop as a major air cargo centre and specialist operators included Lloyd International and Transmeridian, the latter flying the swing-tailed CL-44s — three of which are shown here at the airline's hangar in 1979 along with a DC-8 freighter. About this time Transmeridian merged with Gatwick-based IAS Air Cargo to become British Cargo Airlines but the new company collapsed the following year making a substantial dent in Stansted's cargo movements. However, the cargo connection is maintained today by Heavilift Cargo Airlines whose fleet of Belfast freighters and other aircraft, including occasional leased An-124s and IL-76s, is based at Stansted. In addition, Federal Express and UPS are also among the many users of a new £4.5 million cargo centre built alongside the latest terminal. *Aerofilms 388046*

Above right:

Stansted: Stansted was taken over by the BAA in 1966, along with Heathrow and Gatwick, and the following year a Government White Paper designated it as the site for London's third airport. The next 20 years served as a classic example of the way major civil engineering projects are hindered at every turn in this country. While France went ahead with the imaginative development of a green field site at Roissy for a third Paris airport, the British indulged in no less than three public inquiries, the

last of which lasted for two years before a final go-ahead was given in 1985. Work started in 1986 on an entirely new terminal complex in the eastern corner of the airfield, connected to the M11 motorway by several miles of specially built dual carriageway. In addition, the terminal incorporates a station which is served by the regular mainline 'Stansted Express', taking approximately 40min for the run into London's Liverpool Street station. The photo shows a BAe 146 of Air UK flying over the new terminal while under construction in 1989 and this airline is now one of the main users of Stansted, offering a scheduled network which covers 12 domestic and international destinations. By 1992 Stansted had risen to be the eighth busiest airport in the UK with around 2.2 million passengers a year. *British Aerospace plc*

Right:

Stansted: An aerial view showing the award-winning terminal building designed by Foster Associates nearing completion in 1990. After check-in formalities in the main building, passengers proceed to their aircraft by means of 'People Movers' running on elevated tracks to two satellite terminals on the apron. Using this system the airport will have a maximum capacity of 8 million passengers a year, but this could be increased to 15 million by the phased construction of two more satellites when required, although such expansion is subject to parliamentary approval. *BAA*

London City: One of the most imaginative British civil engineering projects in recent years has been the conversion of a derelict section of London's docklands into a fully fledged international airport. Initial feasibility studies on the project were started in 1981 and a demonstration landing on a temporarily cleared wharf was made by a Brymon Airways Dash 7 in June of 1982. However, it was not until 1986 that full planning permission was obtained after a public enquiry and construction began in April of that year by John Mowlem & Co, a civil engineering company which holds a major stake in the ownership of the airport. This view of the airport in 1990 shows the runway laid on the old wharves, which have been cleared of warehouses, while the parking apron and terminal building are on the left at the far end. Since this photo was taken, the runway has been slightly extended at the western end to give a total length of 1,199m which permits the use of jet aircraft such as the BAe 146. One of the airport's main problems to date has been the lack of easy surface access. Currently passengers can arrive by BR train at Silvertown in the top left of the picture, or face a circuitous route by road. However, the Docklands Light Railway will shortly open an extension running down the land on the right of the picture with a station to be situated near the road bridge at the top. *Aerofilms 586147*

London City: The ultimate in before and after pictures! This is the present site of London City airport as it was in 1957 when London's docks were still among the busiest in the world. In the foreground is the basin of the King George V Dock while a long line of cargo ships fill the wharves of the Royal Albert Dock in the background. Between them is a long warehouse-covered jetty which has now been cleared to permit the laying down of the airport's runway. *Aerofilms A69842*

London City: Even in the early 1970s the docks were still reasonably busy and the photo shows a cargo liner in drydock in September 1971. The location of the airport's brand new terminal exactly coincides with the position of the drydock while the parking apron now covers the area of the warehouses alongside. In the lower right of the picture is a school which is still open today, the designers of the airport having gone to great lengths to ensure that any disruption due to aircraft noise is minimal. *Aerofilms. A217988*

Right:
London City: London City opened for business on 26 October 1987 with flights by Brymon and London City Airways to Brussels and Paris. Amsterdam and Channel Islands routes were later added, and Flexair began flights to Rotterdam using Do 228s in 1989. However, these short routes could not sustain the airport and London City Airways, and its parent group (British Midland), eventually withdrew in 1991. Fortunately, demonstration flights by a BAe 146 in 1988 showed that jet operations were feasible and approval for these was given in 1991. Today there are services to Switzerland, Germany and Sweden by airlines flying the 146 (including Crossair shown here) with Brussels, Rotterdam and Paris being served by Brymon, Flexair and Air France. *Author*

Above:
London City: The waterside location lends a pleasant aspect to the terminal buildings and ATC tower at the City airport. Inside the modern building are all the facilities expected of an international airport including shops, bars, restaurant and lounges. The airfield ATC unit has no radar, services being provided by Thames Radar based at Heathrow. *Author*

Left:
Battersea: Right from its earliest days the helicopter has been seen by some as the ideal solution to the problem of accessing busy city centres although the realisation of this dream has been difficult to achieve. BEA helicopters made an experimental start in London with services to and from Heathrow using a site on the south bank of the Thames near Waterloo during 1955/56. However, London's first permanent heliport was opened at Battersea by Westland Helicopters in 1959 and this photo, showing a Westland Widgeon, was taken shortly afterwards. The Widgeon was a five-seater civil development of the S-51 Dragonfly which Westland had built for the Royal Navy between 1948 -53. For environmental and safety reasons flights to and from the heliport are normally routed over the Thames and similar constraints have prevented the development of other public heliports, although today several companies have private helipads in and around the city for their own use. *Quadrant Picture Library*

Luton: Situated some 30 miles north of London, Luton airport has developed as a major base for IT operators despite several efforts to increase and expand scheduled services. This has meant that the fortunes of the airport have been prey to the vagaries of the holiday and tour market with a consequent difficulty in planning for the future. In addition, Luton is facing increasing competition from nearby Stansted but the airport is rising to the challenge with a programme of development, which it is hoped will considerably enhance its appeal to airlines and passengers alike.

Improvements will include a new cargo centre, the first phase of which will open in 1993, and an ambitious scheme to build a £200 million road/rail/ air interchange on the east side of the nearby British Rail main line. This would, in effect become the airport terminal and a rapid transit system would connect to the existing terminal which would be redeveloped as departure lounges and retail facilities. This 1990 photo shows the present airport layout with aircraft clustered around the terminal building behind which is one of the hangars belonging to Britannia Airways, Britain's second largest airline and one which has a long association with Luton. The white-roofed hangar and associated buildings in the foreground belong to Monarch Airlines, another major Luton-based airline.

Aerofilms 582745

Luton: Although Luton Corporation purchased the site for development in 1935, it was not until 1938 that it was opened as a fully licensed commercial airport. In the meantime Percival Aircraft had set up a factory on the airfield in 1936 and began private and test flying in 1937. Aircraft produced included the Q6 and Proctor, but during the war the company undertook the construction of Mosquitoes and when peace returned subsequently went on to produce its own designs including the Prentice, Prince and Pembroke. In 1954 the company became part of the Hunting Group. After World War 2 the airport's commercial development was hampered by the lack of paved runways and the absence of customs facilities. However, things began to change in the early 1950s when the concept of inclusive tour (IT) holidays was devised and several charter operators began to fly from Luton including Hunting Clan and Derby Aviation. A new control tower was opened in 1952 but two major events in 1959 did much to boost the airports prospects. The first was the opening of a new concrete 1,650m runway and the other was the opening of the first stages of the M1 motorway which suddenly made the airport easily accessible from both London and the Midlands.This view shows the airport in the late 1950s with the Hunting Percival factory in the background and the control tower to the right.
Countrywide, via Luton Airport

Luton: Luton airport in 1964. The future shape of the airport can be discerned with the beginnings of today's sweeping apron and the single taxiway leading to the runway. Parked by the hangars in the foreground are four Lockheed Constellations belonging to Euravia, an independent airline set up at Luton in 1962 for the express purpose of operating IT flights. In 1964 the airline began replacing the Constellations with ex-BOAC Britannias and changed its name — to Britannia Airways. The hangar on the right had just been completed and belonged to MacAlpine Aviation, another long-term Luton operator.
Aerofilms A138638

Right:
Luton: The boom in the IT market in the 1960s necessitated the construction of new terminal facilities which were completed in 1966. This building was situated on the southeast side of the main apron and replaced the wooden structures which had grown up around the base of the control tower. Passengers using the airport had grown from a mere 25,000 in 1958 to 357,000 in 1966, and would reach almost 2 million in 1970. *Countrywide, via Luton Airport*

Left:
Luton: A view across the main apron in 1969 showing an interesting selection of aircraft and operators. The Britannia in the foreground, and two more in the background, belong to Monarch Airlines which was formed by the Cosmos Tours Group and started operations in 1968. In the centre are two Britannias and two Boeing 737s of Britannia Airways, the latter being the first of their type in the UK and the first time that an IT airline had ordered brand new jet aircraft. Today it is common practice for charter airlines to order new state-of-the-art aircraft, but in 1967 when Britannia ordered the 737, it was regarded as a revolutionary step. On the left of the picture can be seen a BAC-111 of Autair. This airline was subsequently renamed Court Line and ordered Lockheed TriStars for delivery in 1973. However, the collapse of the airline in 1974 had a profound effect on the British IT market in general and Luton Airport in particular. From a total of over 3 million passengers in 1973 the number fell dramatically to under 2 million in 1975, a blow from which the airport has yet to fully recover.
Aerofilms A192717

Above:
Luton: The main runway at Luton (08/26) has today been extended to a length of 2,160m with turning bays at each end. Access is via two taxiways near the midpoint which means that departing aircraft have to backtrack and turn round before taking off — a procedure which severely limits the movement rate at busy periods. As part of the airport's expansion plans the stub taxiway on the right will be extended to the 26 threshold. This runway is equipped with a Category III ILS system which allows suitably fitted aircraft to make automatic approaches in virtually any weather conditions. The 1966 terminal building has been replaced by a new and enlarged building which opened in stages between 1984 and 1990. The proposed new passenger terminal and interchange facility will be built on land adjacent to the white-roofed buildings, part of the Vauxhall motor factory complex, which can be seen on the right just beyond the end of the runway.   *Aerofilms 586904*

Below:

Southend: Southend's position to the east of London and only a short flying time away from destinations such as Ostend and Rotterdam made it a natural point for air services to the continent. Like most municipal airports, it was originally developed in the 1930s and officially opened in 1935 although the site had been used by the RFC in World War 1. The outbreak of war in 1939 saw it requisitioned for use as a fighter base when it was known as RAF Rochford. By the end of 1944 it was no longer required and was reduced to a care and maintenance basis until derequisitioned at the end of the war. In the 1950s and 1960s Southend was one of the country's busiest airports, resident airlines including Channel Airways and British United Air Ferries, the latter formed from a merger of Silver City and Channel Air Bridge. A major tenant was Aviation Traders Engineering, owned by Freddie Laker and established in 1949, which at one time grew to be the biggest aviation maintenance organisation in the UK. This photo was taken around 1967 and shows the layout of the airfield with the two runways which were laid down by Southend Corporation after the war as, unusually, the RAF made no such improvements during their occupation. *Aerofilms A179228*

Right:

Southend: A common sight at Southend in the 1960s was the Aviation Traders ATL.98 Carvair, a modification of the DC-4 produced to supplement and replace the Bristol Freighters of Channel Air Bridge. This aircraft (G-ANYB) was the first of 21 conversions carried out between 1960 and 1968 and was eventually scrapped in 1970. Channel Air Bridge was formed as a member of the Airwork Group in 1959 and used its Carvairs on long-range routes carrying five cars plus passengers to Strasbourg and Basle. The airline became part of the British United Group in 1960 and that title can be seen on the fin of the aircraft, below the CAB logo. When BUA took over Silver City in 1962, the combined fleet flew as British United Air Ferries. Behind the tail of the Carvair can be discerned a Viking belonging to Tradair, another Southend-based airline which was formed in 1957 and flew extensive charter services from the airport until it was taken over by Channel Airways in 1962. These and other airlines flew a total of 33,884 air transport movements at Southend in 1963, making it the busiest commercial airport on the UK mainland apart from Heathrow. *Quadrant Picture Library 43579*

Right:

Southend: After the heady days of the 1960s, Southend has steadily lost traffic as other airports such as Gatwick, Luton and Stansted have developed. At the time of writing (late 1992) it seems likely that the airport will close down by 1994 unless the owners, Southend Corporation, can find a buyer who is willing to continue running the site as an airport. In 1988, when this photo was taken, scheduled services and charters were still being flown although passenger throughput had fallen to 95,000 compared to a peak of almost 700,000 in 1967. Visible on the apron are several Viscounts of British Air Ferries while a Belfast freighter of Heavilift is standing in front of the Aviation Traders hanger. In the background is the 1,600m main runway (06/24) and failure to extend this in the face of local opposition was one reason for the airport's demise. In the foreground is the threshold of the subsidiary runway (15/33) which was closed in 1992 and is now used only as a taxiway.
Aerofilms 532041

Northolt: Northolt began life as an RFC airfield in 1915 and in the interwar years it was one of the RAF's major fighter airfields. In December 1937 No 111 Squadron, then based at Northolt, was the first to receive the new Hurricane fighter. During the Battle of Britain it was one of the vital Sector airfields in No 11 Group, tasked with the defence of London. As the war moved eastwards after D-Day, the airfield was taken over by Transport Command and after the war it was temporarily loaned to the Ministry of Civil Aviation from March 1946 while development went ahead at nearby Heathrow. Prior to the handover considerable work was undertaken including resurfacing and lengthening of the runways, and construction of a new control tower

and terminal facilities. From 1946 it became the centre of BEA's operations until flights were gradually transferred to Heathrow in the early 1950s. BEA's last commercial flight, a DC-3 to Jersey, took place on 30 October 1954 after which the airfield reverted to RAF use. Today it is used mainly for military and government VIP flights, although civil aircraft may also fly in with prior approval. The aerial photo was taken in 1955, just after the cessation of civil flying and what was the airport terminal and apron area can be seen on the south side of the airfield, convenient for the main A40 road which runs along the southern boundary. The RAF hangars and other station buildings are on the north side. *Aerofilms A55729*

Croydon: Prior to World War 2, Croydon Airport in Surrey was Britain's premier international airport and by 1939 it was the base for Imperial Airway's landplane fleet which flew extensive services throughout Europe and the Empire. In addition it was served by most of the contemporary European airlines as shown in this 1935 photo of a Savoia Marchetti S73 belonging to the Belgian state airline, Sabena, parked in front of the terminal building and control tower (built in 1928). The three-engined S73 had first flown in 1934 and could carry up to 18 passengers over a distance of 600 miles.

During World War 2 most civil airlines were transferred to Whitchurch Down (Bristol) and the airfield was initially used by Hurricane squadrons until after the Battle of Britain when it was utilised mainly for training and transport operations. After 1945 the lack of hard runways limited its usefulness and its importance as a civil airfield rapidly declined. The opening of nearby Gatwick in 1958 spelt the end and Croydon officially closed in September 1959. *Quadrant Picture Library 14702*

Croydon: The interior of Croydon's control tower in 1935 naturally seems old fashioned when compared to modern ATC facilities but, at the time, it was considered to be among the most advanced in the world. In most cases contact with aircraft was through radio operators in an adjacent room who used W/T to pass and receive messages by morse code. Many of the commonly used code groups still form part of the modern aviation vocabulary, examples including QNH (sea level atmospheric pressure), QTE (true bearing) and QDM (magnetic direction to steer). The control officers would plot the position of each aircraft on the map using information received from radio reports and from bearings obtained by a number of radio D/F stations situated in southeast England. In addition to aircraft taking off and landing at Croydon, they also provided a service to aircraft flying in an area roughly bounded by Croydon, Southend, Manston, Lympne and Bexhill which was known as the London-Continent Airway. *GEC-Marconi*

Heston: London's other major airport prior to World War 2 was Heston, just northeast of the present Heathrow. It was opened as a private airfield by Airwork Ltd in July 1929 and progressively developed over the next 10 years. Customs facilities were provided in 1931, a new large hangar was completed in 1936 and the terminal was extended in 1939. The latest flying aids, including a Lorenz Beam approach system, were also installed. Commercial users included Jersey Airways, Spartan Airlines and United Airways, the latter two merging in 1936 to become British Airways, who then moved to Gatwick, returning the following year due to the unsatisfactory state of the other aerodrome. In 1931 the Kings Cup Air Race was held at Heston and the photograph probably depicts that occasion. Included in the range of airport buildings are the control tower, administrative offices, a hotel and a restaurant — altogether an extremely advanced complex for the time. *CAA*

Heston: An Avro 616 Avian IVM with a smartly attired porter carrying the pilot's baggage to his waiting car. Not many airports offer this level of service today! In 1938 Heston was taken over by the Government and it was here that Neville Chamberlain landed after his meeting with Hitler at Munich in 1938, bearing his infamous piece of paper and declaring 'Peace in our time'. The airfield was also used by Fairey Aviation and it was also here that Sidney Cotton pioneered the use of high performance aircraft (initially a Lockheed 12 Electra) for high altitude photographic reconnaissance, flying unhindered over Germany right up to the outbreak of war. After use by the RAF during World War 2, Heston's career was brief and flying ceased in 1946 due to the development of adjoining Heathrow. Although an aviation connection existed for many years as the buildings were used as offices by the Ministry of Aviation and CAA well into the 1970s. Today the control tower and other buildings have been demolished and the airfield site is bisected by the M4 motorway. *Aerofilms A5405*

Below:

Biggin Hill: Biggin Hill must be one of the most evocative locations in British aviation history. First used by the RFC in 1917, it became one of the RAF's premier fighter airfields between the wars and saw considerable action during the Battle of Britain. It was one of the first RAF airfields to have paved runways, the work being completed shortly after the outbreak of war. After 1945 it remained as an operational RAF station until 1959 when Surrey Aviation was granted a lease of the South Camp, although the RAF retained the North Camp which included the well known Aircrew Selection Centre. During the postwar period Biggin was home to No 600 (City of London) Squadron, RAuxAF, and one of their Meteor F.8 aircraft is shown here in 1952 during Exercise Ardent. In common with the other Auxiliary squadrons, No 600 disbanded in 1957. *Quadrant Picture Library 27817*

Overleaf top:

Biggin Hill: Since 1959 Biggin Hill has grown to become London's largest and busiest general aviation airfield. The 1,800m main runway means that the largest executive jets can use the airfield and full ATC (no radar) and customs facilities are provided. In addition, there are at least a dozen flying schools and clubs as well as significant numbers of privately owned aircraft. The current owner is the London Borough of Bromley which runs the airfield through Biggin Hill Airport Ltd. Although lacking the money to develop the airport to its full potential, Bromley council has expressed its intention to ensure that this valuable asset remains available as a major aviation centre. This view of the airport was taken in 1973 and although there have been various developments since then, the basic layout remains the same. The South Camp is on the left of the main runway (03/21) and the North Camp, now completely vacated by the RAF, is on the right. A major new tenant in 1992 is Metair, part of the Hunting Group, which has moved into a £7 million centre which will be used for fitting out Saab 340s under contract to the manufacturer, and the airport is actively encouraging the growth of other similar aviation-related activities *Aerofilms 280589*

Right:
Biggin Hill: The former 1950s ex-RAF control tower building is the centre of operations at the airfield which is now run by Airports UK. The extension on the left houses a small but comfortable executive lounge for use by business passengers. At the time of writing it appears that Biggin Hill is set to receive its first scheduled passenger service with daily flights from Carlisle due to commence in 1993. These will be flown by Newair, a Newcastle-based airline, using 19-seater Jetstreams. *Author*

Blackbushe: In the postwar period Blackbushe was one of London's major airports and was a base for many independent airlines and charter companies. The site was developed as a military airfield during 1941 and was originally known as Hartfordbridge. It subsequently became the headquarters of No 2 Group and was home to a wing of Boston tactical bombers for some time before and after the Normandy invasion in 1944. In the closing months of the war Blackbushe was transferred to Transport Command and became a base for flights by both military and civil aircraft operating to the continent. The airport was comprehensively equipped with the latest landing aids, including FIDO fog dispersal equipment. This remained when the airport was handed over to the Ministry of Civil Aviation in 1947 and is shown here during a demonstration staged in 1952 after it had been overhauled. In fact there appears to be only one recorded use of FIDO by a civil aircraft in all the years it was installed. During the 1950s Blackbushe was used, among others, by Airwork, Britavia, Silver City, Skyways, Dan Air, Eagle Airways (later British Eagle), while the US Navy used it as their London base and their R4D-8s (Super DC-3), R5D Skymasters and R6D Liftmasters were a common sight. Blackbushe was also a major departure point for numerous trooping flights due to its proximity to the major Army bases at Aldershot and on Salisbury Plain. However, the development of Heathrow and Gatwick made Blackbushe less important, and its operation posed ATC problems for Heathrow. Consequently the government closed the airfield in 1960 and aviation activities ceased until it was partially reopened in 1962. In 1973 it was sold to Douglas Arnold who later erected new hangars and used the airfield as a base for his well known repair and restoration of World War 2 aircraft. This 1975 photo shows the original layout of the airfield but since that time the subsidiary runways have been closed and flying takes place from the 1,350m main runway (08/26) and a grass strip running alongside.
Aerofilms 311429

Above:
Elstree: Elstree airfield, just north of London, has always been a centre for private flying since it opened in the 1930s as an adjunct to a local country club. It saw little military use in World War 2 but was used by Handley Page as a satellite to their main airfield at Radlett, only four miles away. This photo was taken in the early 1960s and shows an Avro 19 Series 2 (civil Anson) and Chipmunks of the London School of Flying parked by the hangars on the south side of the airfield. The small single storey white building just by the tail of the Avro is the control tower. This aircraft (G-AGWE) was previously owned by the Decca company who used it for the development and demonstration of the Decca area navigation system. *Aerofilms 122107*

Below:
Elstree: Elstree in 1992 showing a similar area to the previous photo. A third hangar has been added alongside the pair in the centre of the picture but the control tower remains almost unchanged although the wooden building which stood alongside has been demolished. Cabair, whose logo appears on the hangars, is the airfield's major tenant and are owners of the London School of Flying (LSF) which still flourishes. As is common in airfield scenes compared with 30 years ago, the picture is dominated by American-built aircraft while British-built aircraft are now a rarity. Served by a single 656m hard runway, Elstree is currently owned by the Montclare Shipping Co. *Author*

White Waltham: Situated near Maidenhead in Berkshire, White Waltham is operated by West London Aero Services and is home to several flying clubs with over 100 aircraft based on the airfield. It was the de Havilland company which opened the aerodrome when it set up a flying school for training RAF reservists in 1928. In 1935 No 13 EFTS was established, also by de Havilland, and 600 pilots were trained in the years up to 1941 when the airfield became the headquarters of the Air Transport Auxiliary (ATA), responsible for ferrying new aircraft from factories to various RAF and FAA units. After the 1945 White Waltham became the headquarters for RAF Home Command which, among other tasks, was responsible for the running of the popular Air Training Corps. The RAF station,

situated on the south side of the airfield, closed in 1973 but another major tenant was Fairey Aviation which moved here after the war when development at Heathrow led to the closure of its previous base at Heston in 1947. Thus White Waltham saw the first flight of several new aircraft over the years including the turboprop Gannet and the exciting, but unsuccessful, Rotodyne VTOL airline. However, the company closed down during the restructuring of the aircraft industry in the 1960s and the factory buildings have been put to other uses. The photo shows White Waltham as it is today with an impressive line up of aircraft outside the West London Aero Club premises on the east side of the airfield. *West London Aero Services.*

Top:
White Waltham: A visit to White Waltham in 1960 would have produced a fascinating cross-section of light aircraft then common on the British register, such as Austers, Tiger Moths, Chipmunks, and Geminis. Unusual, even for those days, was this de Havilland DH.85 Leopard Moth shown here with its wings folded. Given the premium on hangar space at most airfields, this is a feature which would be popular today! The small hangar in the immediate background has been replaced by a larger structure, but the blister hangars and wooden clubhouse, visible in the distance, remain almost unchanged today. *Author*

Above:
White Waltham: Another 1960 view of White Waltham showing a newly delivered Beagle Terrier, a three seater converted from ex-Army Auster AOP.6 aircraft. In the background are the buildings of the Fairey Aviation factory, while a London UAS Chipmunk taxies past an RAF runway control caravan. *Author*

Below:
Booker: Wycombe Air Park, otherwise known as Booker, is another of the busy general aviation airfields serving the London area. It was originally opened up as Marlow Airport in 1939 but was immediately requisitioned by the Air Ministry and used as a base for No 21 EFTS which was operated by Airwork Ltd under contract. This unit, flying Tiger Moths, Oxfords, Harvards and Austers, continued flying well after the war and disbanded in 1949. It was replaced, in 1951, by No 1 Basic Flying Training School flying Chipmunks (also operated by Airwork) and the photo shows the airfield at that time. Other units included the London University Air Squadron and the Bomber Command Communications Flight, used to convey staff to and from the nearby Command HQ at High Wycombe. In the mid-1960s the airfield passed into civil ownership and has since developed as a base for several flying and gliding clubs. Booker is also the home of Personal Plane Services who specialise in the building of replica aircraft and the repair and restoration of a variety of interesting types. This company has been much involved in film work and has recently opened a museum at the airfield displaying many of the aircraft and other items of aeronautica used in films such as *The Blue Max. Quadrant Picture Library 25768*

Redhill: Situated a few miles north of Gatwick, Redhill is very much in the shadow of the international airport with many restrictions on the operation of its aircraft. Even when first opened, in 1934, it was similarly restricted by the operations of nearby Croydon. In the war it was used mostly for training purposes and during this period a tarmac perimeter track, still in use, was laid down. After 1945 it returned to civil use and became home of the legendary Tiger Club which remained here for many years before transferring to Headcorn in Kent, away from the restrictions of operating close to the London and Gatwick control zones. This view shows the north corner of Redhill in 1967 and several of the Tiger Club's aircraft are parked on the grass near the control tower, which today has been replaced by a newer structures and small terminal on another part of the airfield. Also visible is a Hiller 12E of Bristow Helicopters who set up their headquarters here in 1958 and remain today. In fact Redhill is now used for a regular international helicopter industry show which attracts visitors from all over the world. The airport has recently announced proposals to lay down a paved runway and upgrade ATC facilities in order to provide an alternative site for executive aircraft wishing to avoid high charges at Gatwick. *Aerofilms 167044*

Denham: Denham is a privately-owned airfield situated a few miles northwest of Heathrow and is just inside the boundary of the London Control Zone. The site saw use as a training airfield during World War 1 but flying ceased during the 1920s. In 1929 the fledgling Martin Baker company set up a manufacturing facility here although any flight testing was carried out at Chalfont. However, the owner of the land, Mr J. Myles Bickerton, used it as an airfield for his Miles Hawk and allowed a few other owners to base their aircraft here. A nearby country club provided a suitable ambience in those halcyon days of British light aviation in the 1930s. During World War 2 the airfield was requisitioned and used as a relief landing ground for Booker and also for glider pilot training. After 1945 the airfield reverted to its original owner and it gradually

became a busy general aviation airfield with several resident clubs and air taxi operators. One of the most successful of these was Air Gregory (née Gregory Air Taxis) which was formed in 1963 and operated a fleet of Aztecs and Twin Commanches as well as a Luton-based HS125 until it was taken over by the Bristol Street Group and the air taxi side was then run down. Today, the airfield is home to the Denham School of Flying (part of the Cabair Group) and the Denham Cessna Flight Centre, as well as a number of other aviation concerns including European Helicopters whose hangar is one of several shown in this photo of the north side of the airfield. There is a 779m tarmac runway (06/24) although the grass areas are also used for take-off and landing. *Aerofilms 572891*

Above:
Fairoaks: Another of the busy general aviation airfields serving the capital, Fairoaks is only a few miles southwest of Heathrow. Flying started here before the war and it became a base for an Elementary and Reserve Flying Training School run by Universal Air Services. It continued in the training role as an RAF station until 1953 when it closed down and it was not until 1957 that it was sold by the government and reopened for civil flying. In recent years an 800m tarmac runway has been laid down and the airport is host to a number of thriving concerns including Alan Mann Helicopters, GAMA Aviation, Merlix Air and Star Aviation as well as the Fairoaks Flight Centre. This view of the airfield was taken in 1989. *Aerofilms 558421*

Right:
Fairoaks: A section of the parking apron at Fairoaks with the control tower in the background. *Author*

2. Birmingham, Wales and The Midlands

Birmingham: An excellent aerial view of the new Eurohub terminal which opened in July 1991 and was designed in association with British Airways and Birmingham European Airways. Eurohub's unique concept is that it houses facilities for domestic and international flights within a single complex enabling passengers from various UK airfields to transfer with the minimum of formalities to departing international flights, which are carefully timed to provide connecting services. Domestic destinations served by Eurohub flights include Aberdeen, Belfast, Edinburgh, Glasgow and Newcastle and there are onward flights to no less than 17 European cities. The main terminal in the background continues to support other scheduled operators as well as a substantial charter programme. One of its major features is the unique Maglev shuttle which connects the terminal to the British Rail main line station and the National Exhibition Centre. Birmingham International Airport expects to cater for over 10 million passengers a year by the end of the century and at least a quarter of these will pass through the Eurohub terminal. *Birmingham International Airport*

Right:
Birmingham: A staged publicity photo taken shortly after Birmingham's Elmdon airport opened in May 1939. Previously the city had been served by Castle Bromwich airfield which was owned by the Air Ministry and which had become the site of a massive shadow factory for Spitfire production. The design of the new terminal, with its overhanging canopies was influenced by Berlin's Tempelhof airport and remains unique for a British airport. The aircraft in this picture is a Percival Q6 of Western Airways Ltd and was used on services linking Birmingham with Bristol, Cardiff and Weston-super-Mare. Carrying up to six passengers, the Q6 was an attractive aircraft and a total of 27 were built of which only four had retractable undercarriages as fitted to the aircraft in this picture (probably G-AFIX). *Birmingham International Airport*

Left:

Birmingham: During World War 2 Elmdon was taken over by the Air Ministry and was mainly used for test flying of Lancaster and Stirling bombers built at various midland factories, including one run by the Austin company situated adjacent to the present NEC site. The airfield was also home to No 14 Elementary Flying School and literally thousands of pilots received their training here. In order to cope with the large bombers two tarmac runways were laid down during the war and a two additional hangars were erected alongside the original No 1 hangar. All three can be seen in this 1965 photo of the south area which also shows a new extension, opened in 1961, to the right of the original terminal building. In the early 1960s the apron area was extended, as can be seen from the area of freshly laid concrete, and the multi-storey car park behind the hangars was opened in 1965. The No 3 hangar on the left was demolished in 1987 for safety reasons as it was too close to the runway for modern all-weather operations. *Aerofilms 150261*

Above:

Birmingham: The approach control radar room at Birmingham in 1962. Second from the right is the approach procedural controller with the approach radar controller on his left looking at the display of the Marconi 264 radar which he would use for sequencing aircraft on to final approach. Immediately to his left is the circular dial and pointer of the D/F equipment. The controller on the left of the picture is sitting in front of the twin displays of the Decca (later Plessey) 424 approach radar which was mainly used to provide Surveillance Radar Approaches (a form of talkdown) to aircraft not equipped with ILS. The 424 radar was a popular installation at many smaller airports at that time where it was often the only radar available. Due to the fact that the radar beam was very fine and the controller had continuously to adjust the aerial setting in order to track aircraft as they approached the airfield, and the short wavelength of the radar pulses meant that it was adversely affected by weather clutter, the 424 required a high degree of skill to use it efficiently. This photo has been lit by the flashgun, but normally the room would be completely darkened so that the radar screens could be viewed. *Birmingham International Airport*

Left:

Birmingham: Despite the opening of the new terminal, ATC is still housed in the original complex within the old buildings. However, the equipment has been considerably updated as can be seen from this recent photograph. Each controller now has two Cossor 1600 radar displays, which are capable of showing alpha-numeric data derived from the SSR system, and all communications and ancillary equipment is operated by neat rows of backlit push buttons. The small square panel just above the controller's left hand is the Furneau Electronics VDF display which has replaced the massive desk-mounted equipment shown in the previous photo. Above the VDF is the IRVR display which gives a continuous readout of visibility along the runway during periods of fog. *CAA*

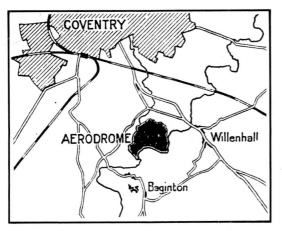

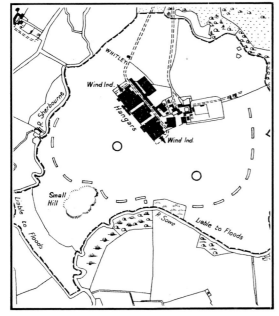

Right:

Coventry: Baginton was opened as Coventry's municipal airport in 1935 but its importance as an air transport centre was overshadowed by the activities of Armstrong Whitworth who, during the war, produced Whitleys and Lancasters, and later went on to build Lincolns, Meteors and Seahawks. In addition, they produced the prototype Apollo turboprop airliner in 1949 and later the four-engined Argosy transport aircraft. Surprisingly, despite the hundreds of aircraft produced, a paved runway was not laid until 1960. However, aircraft production ceased in 1965, by which time Armstrong Whitworth had been taken over by Hawker Siddeley and outstanding work was transferred to the nearby Bitteswell factory. By this time Coventry Airport was overshadowed by developments at Birmingham and consequently it was difficult to persuade airlines to start up alternative operations. However, over the years there have been a few services including a BUAF car ferry service to Calais and British Midland to Jersey. Home-based airlines included Air Commuter, who started a Paris service in 1982 and later became Venture Airways using a HS.748, but operations ceased in 1984. At one time, in the early 1980s, serious consideration was given to closing the airport down, but enough traffic has been generated to persuade the council to improve the facilities and keep going. The photo was taken in 1990 and shows the jumble of buildings which contain ATC and the airport administration. *Author*

Below right:

Coventry: One of Coventry's major customers is Air Atlantique whose main base has been here since 1986. The airline's vintage DC-3s and DC-6 freighters are a common sight and dwarf the numerous light aircraft which are also based on the airfield. Scheduled flights are still flown by Air Corbière, a commuter airline flying Cessna Caravan IIs, while other residents include Dollar Helicopters who carry out all maintenance on their fleet at Coventry. In addition to the main 1,615m runway 05/23, a 800m subsidiary runway (17/35) was opened in 1992, which will be of considerable benefit to the several flying schools which use the airport. Of interest to enthusiasts is the Midland Aircraft Museum situated on the northern boundary which contains an extensive collection of aircraft, including several housed in a purpose-built hangar. *Author*

Above:

Coventry: The development of Coventry's airport at Baginton, three miles southeast of the city, owes much to the activities of the Armstrong Whitworth company which had built its first factory by a small airfield at Whitley Abbey, a mile or so north of Baginton. However, by the mid-1930s, the company was engaged in the design and construction of larger aircraft, such as the AW.23 and the Whitley bomber, and it became obvious that the airfield at Whitley was much too small. This plan well illustrates the problems, showing the restricted landing area and the natural hazards which surrounded it. It was, therefore, decided that a new factory would be built at Baginton and the subsequent transfer of production facilities began in 1936, although the Whitley factory itself did not close down until the end of the war.

Above:
East Midlands: East Midlands Airport, conveniently situated just off the M1 motorway between Nottingham and Derby, is the only one of Britain's major airports to have been built from scratch since the end of the war. It was not quite the first all-new airfield, that distinction going to Ferryfield in Kent, but it is certainly the most successful. In fact the Castle Donington site had previously been used briefly in World War 1 and again between 1943 and 1946 when it was a Bomber and Transport OTU. However, it then lay disused and when, in 1964, work started on the new East Midlands Airport, virtually everything including the runway and taxiways had to be built from scratch. The new airport was officially opened by HRH The Duke of Edinburgh in April 1965, an event shown in this photograph. In 1966, its first full year of operation, almost 130,000 passengers used the airport, many of them carried by British Midland who set up their operating base here. *East Midlands Airport*

Below:
East Midlands: Apart from the new terminal, the airport also had the foresight to provide large hangars which could be used for heavy engineering and this persuaded Fields Aircraft Services to move in. Today this establishment at the west end of the airfield has grown considerably and also includes British Midland's maintenance facilities while in the foreground is the Britannia Airways Cabin Crew recruitment and training centre. The aircraft in the centre of the picture is a Merchantman freighter of Air Bridge Carriers (recently renamed Hunting Cargo Airlines) who are a major user of the extensive cargo and warehousing facilities sited to the east of the terminal. In the background is the main runway which was extended from its original 1,800m to its present 2,280m during the early 1980s. *East Midlands Airport*

Left:

East Midlands: The terminal building at East Midlands was built in 1965 and has since been extended to cope with the 1.2 million passengers a year using the airport. Scheduled services are provided by several airlines including British Midland, Aer Lingus and Business Air. Charter operators include Britannia, Inter European, Excalibur and Air Malta. *Author*

Below left:

East Midlands: The proximity of the Rolls Royce factory at Derby often results in unusual aircraft visiting East Midlands and a typical example is this RB-211-powered Russian Tupolev Tu-204 which paid a fleeting visit after the 1992 Farnborough Air Show. Rolls Royce also use East Midlands to fly out RB-211 engines to customers around the world. *Author*

Below:

East Midlands: A plan of East Midlands showing the layout of the terminal area and maintenance facilities to the south of the main runway. For the long term, the airport planners are looking at the possibility of a second terminal to cater for increasing demand, and this could be sited on the other side of the runway. An interesting innovation is the setting up of an aircraft museum and information centre adjacent to Hold B at the eastern end of the airfield. *CAA*

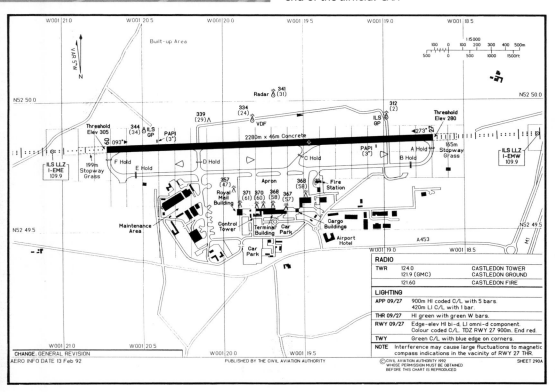

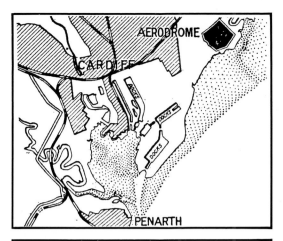

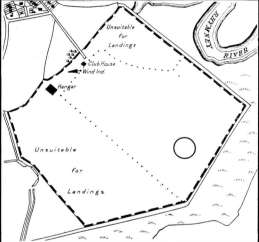

Cardiff: Cardiff Wales airport at Rhoose is now a major regional airport but, for many years, Cardiff was served by the small municipal airport at Pengham Moors situated only two miles to the east of the city centre. Opened in 1931, this was subsequently used by airlines such as GWR Air Services, the British Air Navigation Co and Western Airways serving a variety of destinations including Bristol, Birmingham, Plymouth and Liverpool, as well as occasional flights to Paris. During the war the airfield was requisitioned and used mainly as a dispatch point for preparing aircraft due to be shipped overseas through nearby Cardiff Docks. A 870m concrete runway was laid down in 1942. After the war Pengham returned to civil use although the RAF retained a presence through No 3 Reserve Flying School. Services were operated by BEA, Cambrian Air Services and Western Airways, but the short runway precluded any major development and all civil flying transferred to Rhoose in 1954. The plan shows Pengham Moors in its prewar layout before the addition of a concrete runway.

Right:
Cardiff: Rhoose took over as Cardiff's civil airport in 1954, although Aer Lingus had been using the airfield since 1952 for their Dublin service flown by DC-3s. Built during 1941/42, Rhoose was used by No 53 OTU with Spitfires and was later the base for No 7 Air Gunnery School. After the war it served briefly as a Maintenance Unit before it was eventually taken over by the MTCA and developed as a civil airport. For many years it was the base of Cambrian Airways which, in 1972, was absorbed into British Airways, surviving for a few years as a regional division of the state airline. Meanwhile, in 1965, the airport was transferred to Glamorgan County Council and renamed Glamorgan (Rhoose) but since 1978 has been officially known as Cardiff Wales, reflecting its status as the Principality's only major regional airport. The main runway (12/30) was extended to a length of 2,354m in 1970 while a new terminal, sited on the north side of the airfield, opened in 1972. This photo shows passengers disembarking from an Aer Lingus Viscount parked by the old terminal to the south of the main runway during 1969. The control tower visible in the background was completed in that year and is still in use but has been incorporated into the structure of the latest developments. *Cardiff Wales Airport.*

Below right:
Cardiff: This 1988 photo shows the new terminal sited on the north side of the main runway. The layout features two piers serving parking stands for up to a dozen large aircraft and the control tower has been incorporated into the westerly of these. The long white building to the right of the terminal is a purpose built cargo centre and over 7,000 tons of freight was carried in 1991/92 in addition to half a million passengers. Since British Airways withdrew from the routes previously served by Cambrian, the airport has had varying success in attracting other airlines to operate scheduled services. Currently Manx Airlines are setting up a major operation which will be based around new Jetstream 41s on order from British Aerospace. Cardiff is also the base of Inter European Airways, which flies an extensive charter programme with a fleet of Boeing 737s and 757s, while other airlines fly charters to European and trans-Atlantic destinations. A significant recent addition is the construction of a massive hangar on a 70 acre site just to the west of the threshold for runway 21. Just visible in the top left hand corner of this picture, the new hangar will form part of a multi million pound British Airways maintenance facility occupying a 70 acre site. Known as project Dragonfly, the facility will employ around 1,200 people and will carry out major engineering work on all aircraft in BA's fleet, including the largest 747s. The reopening of the taxiway from the main apron to the BA hangar site has meant that the aircraft museum has been relocated to a new site adjacent to the airport access road (top centre). *Cardiff Wales Airport.*

Derby: Burnaston was established as an airfield in 1938 with an RAF ERTS and the Derby Aero Club both based here. The following year it was formally opened as Derby's municipal airport and was then almost immediately requisitioned on the outbreak of war, when it continued as a base for various training activities including, from 1942, pilots for the Army's Glider Pilot Regiment. When peace came the airfield quickly reverted to civil use, although No 3 Basic Flying Training School continued using Burnaston until 1953. In the meantime Derby Aviation was formed in 1949 and flew charter services with a Rapide and Miles Aerovan. Subsequently the company expanded considerably and eventually became British Midland Airways in 1964. The activities of Derby Aviation and its fleet of DC-3s, Marathons and Argonauts played havoc with the airport's grass surface and consequently the airline, in its new BMA guise, moved all its activities to the new airport at East Midlands as soon as it opened in 1965. Flying operations at Burnaston then ceased for several years. This photo was taken in 1962 and shows the airfield bordering the main A38 trunk road in the foreground. The entire Derby Airways fleet of Argonauts appears to be parked by the hangars. *Aerofilms A102219*

Derby: During the 1980s Derby had a brief renaissance as a private airfield used by the Derby Aero Club and other private owners. The club premises which also acted as the airfield operations centre are shown here in 1989. *Author*

Derby: In 1990 Derby became the second airfield in recent times to be redeveloped as a site for a car factory, the other example being Usworth (Sunderland). In Derby's case the new arrival was another Japanese company, Toyota, who have built a massive factory on the site — completely obliterating any sign of the previous aviation activities. The only relic which is apparent is a mushroom-type pillbox, one of several which were part of the airfield's wartime defences, which stands in a loop of the flyover which now leads off the A38 into the Toyota premises. The same pillbox can be discerned in the aerial photo, standing in the small light coloured field on the left of the A38 as it passes the airfield boundary. Readers will be pleased to note that the Derby Aero Club have recently been granted planning permission to open an alternative airfield at nearby Egginton Junction. *Author*

Top:
Nottingham: Tollerton was officially opened as Nottingham's municipal airport in June 1930 and this photograph was taken some three years later. A typical grass airfield of the time, the facilities included a hangar and administrative building which can be seen on the left. In the centre of the landing area is a standard 50ft diameter white circle with the airport name alongside (these markings were made by digging out the turf to the required shape and filling the resulting depressions with chalk). The longest take-off run was 900yd in a NE/SW direction. During World War 2 the airfield was taken over by the RAF and used as a Flying Training School, and in 1941 three tarmac runways and associated taxiways were laid down. After 1945 Field's Aircraft Services occupied a large hangar, which had been erected on the western side of the airfield, and carried out maintenance work on a wide variety of military and civil aircraft. The Air Ministry relinquished the airfield in 1956 since when it has been privately owned. *Quadrant Picture Library 9047*

Above:
Nottingham: Tollerton today is a busy general aviation airfield owned and operated by Truman Aviation. A modest clubhouse and ATC tower are home to the flying club and provide facilities for visiting pilots. In the background can be seen the roof of the original hangar, while to the left of that is a pub and restaurant which stands on the site of the original terminal building. A new hangar is under construction and when this is complete, the old Field's hangar (not visible in this picture) will be demolished. The 1,056m main runway (09/27) is still in use, while part of R/W 03/21 is also used although there are plans to resurface parts of the latter in order to allow a greater length to be used. The third runway is now used for aircraft parking. *Author*

Above:

Oxford: Oxford's Kidlington airfield is home to the Oxford Air Training School (OATS) which, with a fleet of over 50 aircraft and helicopters, provides comprehensive training courses for student and professional pilots from around the world. In addition the school also trains aircraft engineers and has an impressive range of sophisticated flight simulators. The school began operations in May 1964 and subsequently trained 750 pilots for BEA and BOAC over a five year period. Later customers included Britannia Airways, Japan Airlines and Cathay Pacific. OATS is itself a subsidiary of CSE Aviation who are the owners and operators of the airfield and who provide extensive aircraft engineering facilities as well as acting as sales agents for various aircraft manufacturers including Piper, Embraer, and Schweizer Helicopters. The photo shows one of the school's PA-34 Seneca twin-engined training aircraft parked in front of the airfield's modern ATC Tower and operations centre. *Author*

Below:

Oxford: Kidlington's association with flying training stretches back as far as 1938 when the airfield opened as an RAFVR training unit. During World War 2 it was used for glider pilot training and later for night flying and instrument flight training. After 1945 it reverted to civil use and was run by the Oxford Flying Club before being taken over by Vigor Aviation and, eventually, by CSE. This interesting aerial view was taken in 1960 during an aircraft sales weekend held by W. S. Shackelton Ltd. In the foreground are a fascinating collection of contemporary aircraft including Tiger Moths, Austers, Geminis, as well as an EP-9 and several Miles types. Significantly, on the extreme left of the picture can be seen some of the American light aircraft whose importation was virtually to eliminate the British light aircraft industry. At this time the airfield had a concrete perimeter track, a legacy of the war, but the runways were grass. CSE laid down hard runways (02/20 and 12/30) and replaced the old timber tower and clubhouse with the modern building seen in the other photo. The white hut on the right remains today and is visible by the tail of the Seneca in the other picture. *Quadrant Picture Library 40149*

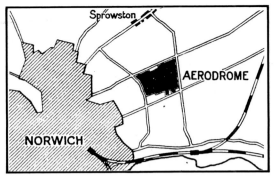

Left:
Norwich: Norwich originally opened its first municipal airport at Mousehold, just to the northeast of the city, in 1933. The site had been used as an aerodrome in World War 1 and was taken over again in 1939, although it seems to have had no operational use and was totally abandoned after the war. This plan shows the layout of the airfield in 1935.

Below:
Norwich: Norwich's present airport is the ex-RAF station at Horsham St Faith. This was built immediately prior to World War 2 and it was here that the first operational Mosquito squadron was formed in 1942. Transferred subsequently to the USAAF it reverted to RAF control again in 1945, and as a Fighter Command base it was successively home to squadrons of Meteors, Hunters and Javelins until flying ceased in the mid-1960s It was purchased by Norwich and Norfolk councils in 1967, but it was not until 1970 that the airport was officially opened as a fully licensed and operational concern. An early arrival was Air Anglia, formed in 1970 by the merger of several smaller charter companies, which set up its headquarters here in 1970. Over the years it grew considerably and, in 1980, as a result of further mergers, it became part of Air UK. In the meantime the airport has steadily developed with improvements to the control tower made in 1977, a new terminal building opened in 1988, a freight transit shed completed in 1989, further terminal extensions opened in 1990 and a new control tower and radar installation sited on the north side of the airfield has just been completed in 1992. *CAA*

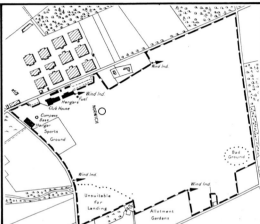

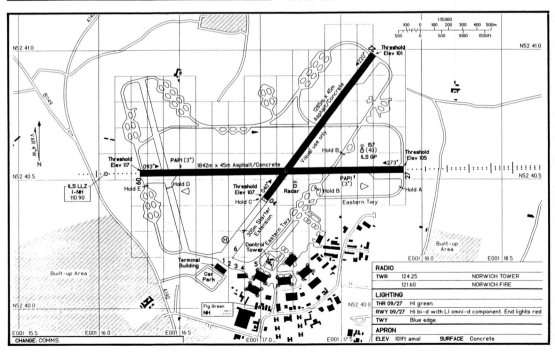

Top:
Peterborough/Conington: For a city of its size, Peterborough must be unique in having two airports, although neither of them is very large. The more commercial of these is at Conington, seven miles south of the city and alongside the BR East Coast main line, and is known as Peterborough Business Airport. The current operator is Klingair who run a busy flying school as well as an aircraft sales and engineering facility. Originally named Glatton, the airfield was built in 1943 as an American 8th Air Force base for the 457th Bombardment Group but closed down in 1946 after the war and reverted to agricultural use, virtually all the wartime buildings being removed or demolished. Since reopening, the remaining hangar has been extended although the control tower is housed in one of several portakabins stacked alongside. Only approximately half of the original 1,800m main runway is available for use today and the two shorter runways are completely disused. In addition to the Klingair fleet, several private and business aircraft are based here. *Author*

Above:
Peterborough/Sibson: Peterborough's other airfield is Sibson, situated six miles west of the city and just off the A1 trunk road. This small grass airfield opened in 1940 as a Relief Landing Ground for the Advanced Flying Training Unit at Peterborough airfield (now closed) and continued in this role until closure in 1946. Subsequently, it was used for private flying and, in recent years, it has blossomed as a centre for sport parachuting under the auspices of the British Parachuting Association. The wartime blister hangars were demolished but two more were subsequently erected including this one which is mainly used for parachute training and has a control tower built on to one side. Sibson has two grass runways, the longer of which is 07/25 (703m). *Author*

Above:

Ipswich: Ipswich municipal airport was officially opened on 26 June 1930 and was used mainly by the Suffolk Aero Club until taken over by the Whitney Straight Corporation in 1936. The new operators implemented a development programme which included an impressive new terminal building opened in 1938 by the Secretary of State for Air. The building was of considerable architectural interest at the time as it represented new trends in modern construction together with the facility for adaptation and expansion to meet changing requirements. However, its peacetime use was all too brief as the airfield was taken over in 1939 for use as an RAFVR Elementary Flying Training School. Later it was used for other tasks, including Blind Approach training and target towing, and, from 1942, it also saw some operational flying as a satellite airfield for Martlesham Heath. The photo shows the airport in the 1930s, prior to the construction of the new terminal and hangar. *Quadrant Picture Library 9370*

Right:
Ipswich: Plan of Ipswich Airport in 1935.

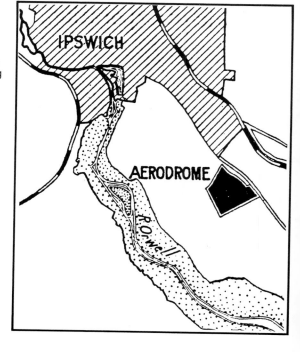

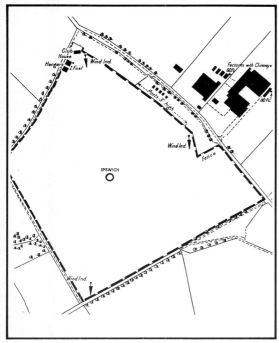

Above:

Ipswich: Ipswich airport today showing aircraft of today's Suffolk Aero Club in front of the 1938 terminal building. The house just visible in the centre background is one of the three which can be seen on the airfield boundary in the previous picture. Since reverting to civil use in 1945, the airport has suffered mixed fortunes. Serious commercial flying revived in 1954 when East Anglian Flying Services, later to become Channel Airways, took over the lease and flew scheduled services to Rotterdam, Southend and the Channel Islands using a variety of aircraft, such as Dragon Rapides, Bristol Freighters and Avro 748s, until their liquidation in 1972. After that a variety of flying schools and aero clubs took over the running of the airport until the lease was taken over by Ipswich Co-operative Society in 1980 with the intention of using it for non-aviation commercial developments. However, with the backing of the council, the airport facilities were upgraded in the mid-1980s by Harvest Air and a new airline, Suckling Airways, was formed with a single Do.228 to fly daily services to Amsterdam. Unfortunately, problems with the grass airfield surface led to Suckling's operations moving to Cambridge and today the Borough Council, the current leaseholders, are seriously considering closure of the site by 1994 for redevelopment.
P.G.Murton

65

3. Manchester and The North

Manchester: Apart from Heathrow and Gatwick, Manchester Ringway is far and away Britain's busiest airport with over 11 million passengers passing through in the 12 months up to July 1992. The next busiest, a long way behind, with around 4.5 million passengers in the same period, is Glasgow while Birmingham trails at 3.5 million. To meet the ever increasing demand Manchester is investing heavily in new developments, several of which are visible in this recent view. At top left is the distinctive red and white £18 million World Freight Terminal which handled 70,000 tonnes of freight in 1991 and at top right is the new international terminal of which the first phase is due to open in 1993 with final completion slated for 1997, when the airport will have a capacity of 23 million passengers a year. In the centre of the picture is the present main terminal with its piers and satellites including a new Domestic Terminal opened in 1989 and a section of the 3,048m main runway is in the foreground.
Aerofilms CH91440

67

Manchester: The Ringway site was not Manchester Corporation's first choice for an airport and it was developed only after problems with the waterlogged site at Barton. In 1934 Fairey Aviation had set up a factory at Ringway and in 1937/38 the airfield was developed as a commercial airport by the construction of a hangar, control tower and passenger terminal in a single combined building. Airline customers included KLM, Railway Air Services and Isle of Man Air Services and, in addition, A. V. Roe also set up a factory on the airfield. During the war Ringway became an important aircraft production centre with the Avro Manchester, Lancaster and York prototypes all making their first flights here, while Fairey produced Fulmars and Barracudas, as well as Beaufighters and Halifaxes under sub-contracts. Several of the latter can be seen here parked around Fairey's hangars on the west side of the airfield in 1946. The still camouflaged terminal building can just be seen in the background on the left. Ringway's other main contribution to the war effort was as a centre for training the glider pilots and parachutists of the Army's airborne forces. Over 60,000 troops passed through the various training establishments between 1940 and 1945. *Aerofilms A799*

Below:
Manchester: The original terminal at Manchester during the 1950s with a Dove and Dragon Rapide of Airviews parked on the apron. This company, and its valuable archive of photographs, has been taken over by Aerofilms of Elstree who have provided so many of the excellent illustrations for this book. In 1949 some of the buildings of the wartime Parachute Training School were converted to handle passengers, supplementing the original terminal which was now too small to cope with the traffic. Later, in 1951, the runway was lengthened to around 1,800m and the following year the number of passengers rose to 163,000. Until 1957 Ringway still saw some military flying as it was the base for the Spitfires and Vampires of No 613 (East Lancashire — City of Manchester) Squadron, RAuxAF, which was finally disbanded in 1957. *Aerofilms B12887.*

Left:
Manchester: Manchester's imposing terminal building, incorporating administration offices and ATC facilities in a multi-storey tower block, was completed in 1962 after four years' work. Two piers provided covered walkways to the aircraft parking stands, only the second such installation in the UK, and further lengthening of the runway was also done at this time. The aerial view of the terminal was taken in 1969 and shows an Andover of the Queen's Flight parked in the foreground, but a more interesting aircraft is the replica Vickers Vimy bomber which had been flown in to take part in celebrations to mark the 50th anniversary of the pioneering trans-Atlantic flight by Alcock and Brown. Tragically, this fine aircraft was destroyed by fire only a few days later while parked on the apron at Manchester, hot sunlight having caused the spontaneous combustion of a section of the freshly doped fabric. *Aerofilms A195315*

Manchester: Throughout the 1960s and 1970s Manchester continued to boom so that further expansion was necessary. A new departure hall was opened in 1973 and was followed in 1974 by a third pier, further terminal extensions and a 20,000 space multi-storey car park. In the 1980s a satellite pier and additional holding lounges were added to the third pier and many of these improvements are visible in this photograph. One reason for the significant increase in passenger traffic was the designation of Manchester by the government as an International Gateway airport. This allowed direct longhaul international flights to be operated and the airport was quick to take advantage of this new status as is shown here with aircraft of Singapore Airlines, Delta, South African Airways and British

Airways all clustered around the satellite and pier. The introduction of wide-bodied aircraft such as the 747 and TriStar also made it necessary to further extend the runway to its present length and this work was completed in 1982. However the airport is now looking for a possible site to build a second runway as the present single main runway reaches saturation point. Originally it was expected that any new runway would be parallel to the present 08/24 but a recent proposal is for it to be built on a east-west axis on a new site to the west of the present airport. Any such development will, of course, be subject to the long and involved planning applications and public inquiries that are inevitable these days. *Manchester Airport plc*

Above:

Manchester Barton: Although now overshadowed by the massive development at Ringway, Barton airfield was Manchester's first airport when it opened in 1929. In fact it was the first municipal airport in the UK to be formally licensed by the Air Ministry, and its D/F equipped purpose-built control tower, completed in 1933, was also the first of its type in the country. Conveniently situated only five miles west of Manchester, the airfield was used by airlines such as Railway Air Services and KLM but flying operations were always hindered by a tendency for the surface to become badly waterlogged after heavy rain despite the use of a cinder bed for the runways. Unusually, the airfield saw little military use in World War 2, although the local firm of F. Hills & Sons built several hundred Percival Proctors for the RAF and these were test flown from the airfield. This aerial view was taken in 1949 and clearly shows the control tower and large brick construction hangar which were both in place before the war. The smaller hangar was a wartime addition.
Aerofilms 22004/49

Right:

Manchester Barton: Barton today is an extremely busy general aviation airfield run by the Lancashire Aero Club. The fine control tower remains almost unaltered, apart from the removal of the tall radio mast, and is surely worthy of preservation as one of the earliest examples of a uniquely 20th century

type of building (in fact it is a Grade 2 listed building and is claimed to be the oldest control tower in the world still in everyday use). Not visible in this photo are two additional hangars erected to house an ever increasing aircraft population. Although this photo was taken in 1992, the biplane parked in front of the tower (a homebuilt Sorrell SNS-7 Hiperbipe) and the Union Jacks fluttering in the summer breeze help to provide an air of nostalgia. Despite Barton's popularity, the future of the airfield is under threat due to a proposed redevelopment of the land which is still owned by Manchester Corporation. *Author*

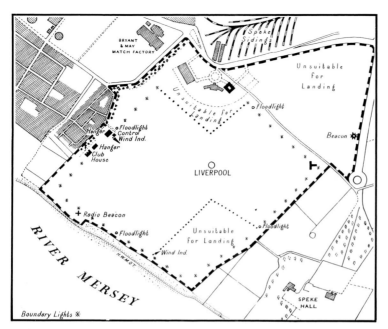

Left:

Liverpool: Liverpool airport, on the banks of the River Mersey, first opened at Speke in 1930 and in the years leading up to World War 2 it became the second busiest in the UK. Full airport status was not attained until 1933 when it was formally licensed by the Air Ministry and customs facilities were established. Early operators included Midland and Scottish Air Ferries, Hillmans Airways, Railway Air Services, KLM and Aer Lingus. In addition, Liverpool and District Aero Club moved from Hooton in 1934 and No 611 (West Lancashire) Squadron, RAuxAF, formed here in 1936. A large hangar was constructed in 1937 along with the six-storey control tower, while the wings of the terminal building were completed in 1939. The plan shows the layout of the airfield in 1937.

Right:

Liverpool: During World War 2 Speke was used for a variety of purposes and a Rootes shadow factory, built alongside in 1938, produced Blenheims and Halifaxes. The proximity of the port of Liverpool led to Speke being used by No 1 Aircraft Assembly Unit which assembled mainly Lockheed aircraft carried across the Atlantic by ship. Another unit with a nautical flavour was the Merchant Ship Fighter Unit which provided the pilots and aircraft to be catapulted off converted merchant ships for the defence of convoys. Interestingly, civil air services to Ireland and the Isle of Man were maintained throughout the war by Railway Air Services and Aer Lingus and as early as September 1944 the airfield was released to the Directorate General of Civil Aviation, and services to London were resumed. After the war the airport saw a brief period of hectic activity as hundreds of American aircraft were flown in to prepare for shipment back to the States. After that, normal commercial operations got underway with BEA using Ju52s for flights to Croydon and Belfast while in 1949 Starways began operations with a DC-3. This airline later grew to own a substantial fleet including Viscounts, but was eventually taken over by British Eagle in 1963 who continued the Liverpool services for a while. The photo shows work underway to extend the parking apron in front of the terminal building in 1948. In the background is the massive No 1 Hangar completed in 1937 while in the foreground is the other main hangar which was completed during the war. An interesting detail here is the mobile GCA (Ground Controlled Approached) radar caravan situated on the track in the lower left hand corner.
Aerofilms A15937

Left:
Liverpool: A close-up of the prewar tower and terminal at Liverpool, which was for many years the most impressive example of airport architecture in the UK. The No 1 Hangar also shows an Art Deco influence. *Aerofilms A69623*

Below:
Liverpool: Somehow Liverpool never regained its prewar position as one of the busiest airports in the UK and slowly lost out to the ever-expanding Manchester Ringway. Ownership of the airport was retained by the government until 1961 when it finally reverted to Liverpool Corporation. In an effort to make up for lost opportunities, a new 2,286m runway (09/27) and a parallel taxiway system was laid down and completed in 1966. By that time Manchester was moving 1.4 million passengers a year – more than three times Liverpool's 450,000 per year. More recently a new terminal and control tower have been built beside the new runway which is located to the east of the original wartime runways. The old terminal closed down in 1986 and, although still standing, is unused. Pictured here is an Il-18 of LOT operating one of the last flights before the move to the new terminal took place. *John Greaves*

Bottom:
Liverpool: A Brymon Airways Dash 7 parked in front of Liverpool's new terminal building after its completion in 1986. Although functional, the new building lacks the interest and grandeur of the older buildings. It is a measure of the problems facing Liverpool that its passenger traffic has remained relatively static over the past 20 years while Manchester's has increased tenfold. In the field of cargo and freight, the airport has fared a little better. For many years it has been the centre of the Post Office's efforts to speed up domestic mail by using aircraft, and a purpose-built mail sorting centre sited adjacent to the terminal is the scene of frantic activity every night. *Adrian Thompson*

Right:
Liverpool: This current plan of Liverpool Airport shows how drastically it has changed in recent years — effectively migrating a mile to the southeast! The main runway and terminal building now comprise the essential heart of the airport while the old runways and buildings to the northwest are virtually disused except that one runway is kept open for use as taxiway access to the old hangar which is still used for maintenance purposes. The operational part of the airfield has now been taken over by British Aerospace, who hope to develop the potential for air cargo, while the original airfield is likely to be redeveloped by Liverpool Corporation. *CAA*

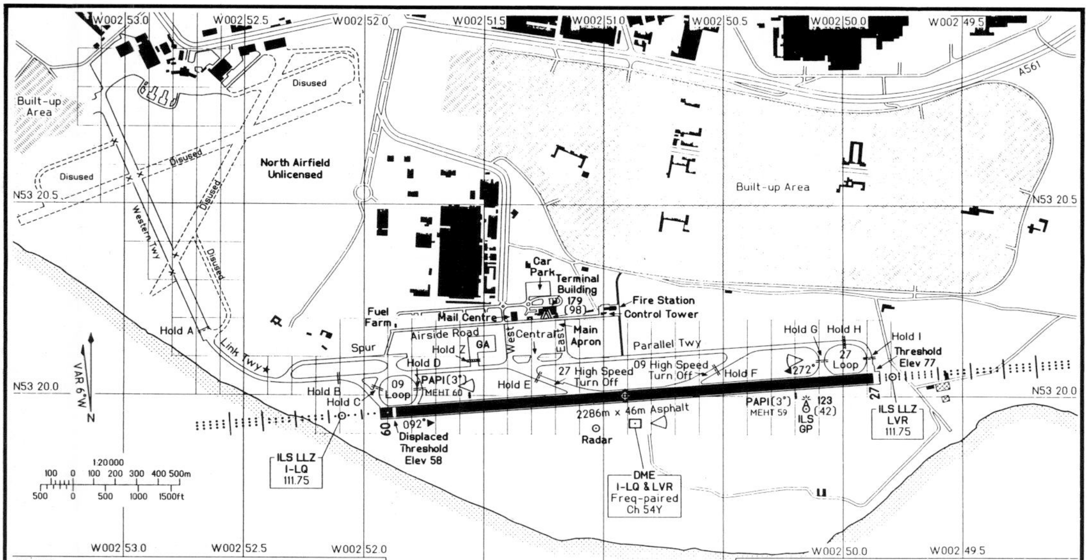

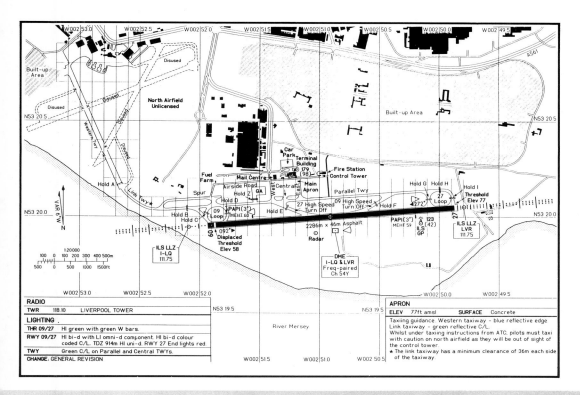

RADIO		
TWR	118.10	LIVERPOOL TOWER

LIGHTING	
THR 09/27	HI green with green W bars.
RWY 09/27	HI bi-d with LI omni-d component. HI bi-d colour coded C/L. TDZ 914m HI uni-d. RWY 27 End lights red.
TWY	Green C/L on Parallel and Central TWYs.

CHANGE: GENERAL REVISION

APRON			
ELEV	77ft amsl	SURFACE	Concrete

Taxiing guidance. Western taxiway - blue reflective edge. Link taxiway - green reflective C/L.

Whilst under taxiing instructions from ATC, pilots must taxi with caution on north airfield as they will be out of sight of the control tower.

★ The link taxiway has a minimum clearance of 36m each side of the taxiway.

Above:
Newcastle: Newcastle's bustling international airport has been steadily expanded in the past decade and, with over 2 million passengers, is now among the top 10 busiest in the UK. Its early days were typical of most municipal airports and the airfield at Woolsington was opened in 1936, replacing a small ex-naval airship field at nearby Cramlington which had previously been used by the local aero club. There was little in the way of commercial flying and the airport was run on behalf of the city by the Newcastle upon Tyne Aero Club, which is still going strong today and claims to be the oldest established aero club in the country. This prewar view shows some of the club's aircraft lined up outside the combined terminal and clubhouse, with the airport's hangar in the background. Although the three DH.60 Moths shown here were late production aircraft, Newcastle Aero Club had been the recipient of two pre-production Moths in 1925 under a scheme where the Air Ministry sponsored the formation of five Moth-equipped clubs.
Newcastle Airport

Left:
Newcastle: Although Woolsington was requisitioned in 1939, it was used only for second line duties and it saw little development. In particular, no paved runways were laid down and, although the airfield was returned to its original owners in 1947, it was not until 1954 that a modest 1,600m runway (07/25) was laid down. In the early 1950s Hunting Clan started scheduled services to London and other destinations using Vikings, DC-3s and, eventually, Viscounts. However, the airline withdrew in 1956 but, in the meantime, BKS had also started operations from Newcastle and by 1959 had established a major presence with daily scheduled flights to London. This photo was taken in the late 1950s and shows a BKS Ambassador on the apron alongside the wooden huts which served as a passenger terminal. In the foreground is the Aero Club and original hangar while a section of the runway can be seen in the background.
Aerofilms 74865

Above:
Newcastle: A photo of the south apron at Newcastle taken in 1989. This area is now used for parking general aviation aircraft and the large hangar is used by Gill Aviation, a locally based commuter airline with a fleet of Shorts 330s and 360s. The Aero Club building and adjacent hangar are virtually unchanged from the 1930s but all terminal and passenger facilities have moved to another part of the airfield. *Author*

Right:
Newcastle: By 1965 some 250,000 passengers were using the airport and the temporary wooden terminal on the south side of the airfield was bursting at the seams. Consequently the go-ahead

was given for an imaginative development, on a site in the northwest corner of the airfield, which comprised a new three-storey terminal with a pier, a new parking apron, cargo facilities and an operations block containing ATC, telecommunications and the airport fire service. In addition, the runway was lengthened to its present 2,332m. While this work was in progress the airfield was closed for a few months in 1965/66 and all operations were temporarily transferred to the nearby RAF airfield at Ouston. The new terminal opened in 1967 and passenger traffic has grown steadily ever since. This view of the main apron in front of the terminal was taken in 1979 and shows a typical selection of aircraft and airlines at that time. The British Airways Trident in the background was one of a fleet of four which had belonged to NorthEast Airlines (the successor to BKS) until taken over by BA in 1973. *Author*

Newcastle: Newcastle International Airport in 1989. The passenger terminal and parking apron are on the left while the maintenance and general aviation facilities are on the right. When this photo was taken the parallel taxiway leading to the far end of the runway had just been completed. Not shown are the radical improvements to the airport's surface access which have been completed in the intervening four years since 1989. In the foreground work is just starting on a dual carriageway which now leads right into the airport, connecting it with the main A1 trunk road. Even more dramatic is the extension of the Tyne and Wear Metro rapid transit system directly into a purpose-built station adjacent to the terminal, linking the airport with the main BR station in Newcastle. Further expansion plans include additional apron space to hold up to five Boeing 757s and the construction of a cargo village on land just to the right of the general aviation apron. *AirFotos via Newcastle Airport*

Above:
Teesside: Teesside Airport, near Middlesbrough, is
a relative latecomer to the ranks of civil airports in
the UK. It was originally built as a Bomber
Command airfield, Middleton St George, in 1941
and was first used by No 78 Squadron flying
Whitleys. Later in the war it was used by Halifax-
equipped RCAF squadrons forming part of No 4
Group. After the war it was used for training
purposes but between 1957 and 1963 it was
extensively upgraded as a Fighter Command airfield
with resident squadrons flying Meteors, Hunters ,
Javelins and Lightnings. However, government
defence cuts in the early 1960s led to the closure of
the airfield and it was sold to a consortium of local
authorities in 1964 for the bargain sum of
£340,000, although a further £1 million was spent
on constructing a terminal and providing other
facilities for commercial operations which
commenced in October of that year. The terminal
was actually opened in 1966 and this photo was
taken in 1969 and shows a pair of BUA BAC-111s
and two BKS Tridents in front of the new facility. In
the background is the airport hotel, converted from
the former RAF Officer's Mess. *Teesside International
Airport*

Left:
Teesside: The ATC control tower at Teesside is one
of many clues to the airport's former role as an RAF
fighter airfield. However, much new equipment has
been added including a Plessey Watchman radar
with its associated display systems. *Author*

Teesside: A pilot's eye view approaching the main 2,291m runway 05/23. Apart from a short section of runway 01/19, the other former RAF runways are used only for parking and taxi-ing. The hangars and terminal area are on the left of the runway and, although not visible, the airport does have its own railway station alongside the distant boundary. One resident on the airfield is the CAA's Fire Training School which trains airport fire-fighters from all over the world. For drill purposes it has several ex-BA Tridents which are parked on the old dispersals in the southeast corner of the airfield. A modest 311,000 passengers used Teesside in the year to July 1992, mostly on scheduled services to London , Aberdeen, Belfast and Amsterdam, although there are a few IT charter flights. However, the airport is a popular venue for airline training flights due to its good facilities and relatively uncrowded airspace, and there are occasional cargo flights. *Teesside Int. Airport*

Right:
Leeds/Bradford: Leeds/Bradford airport, like
Liverpool, has suffered to some extent by virtue of
its proximity to Manchester Airport, but constant
development and investment in new facilities has
helped to keep traffic at a reasonable level. Its
prewar history echoes that of many municipal
airports, opening in 1931 and attracting services
from domestic airlines such as North Eastern
Airways, Blackpool and West Coast Air Services and
Railway Air Services. This plan shows the layout of
the airport then known as Yeadon, as it was in 1935.
From 1936 it also had its own RAuxAF squadron
(No 609 — West Riding) and, following the
outbreak of war, was requisitioned in 1940. Used for
a while by an MU and No 20 EFTS, the airfield was
then taken over by the Ministry of Aircraft
Production to serve a nearby massive shadow
factory which produced 4,800 Ansons and 695
Lancasters. The enormous test flying programme
necessitated the laying down of two runways with
associated hangars and taxiways. After the war, the
airfield passed to the Ministry of Civil Aviation in
1947 but their interest was lukewarm and facilities
were withdrawn in 1953. However, the airport was
reopened under the management of Yeadon
Aviation Services and in 1955 BKS started operations
using DC-3s on routes to Belfast, Jersey, Southend
and the Isle of Wight. BKS went on to become the
major operator at Leeds although other users
included Starways, Aer Lingus and Silver City.

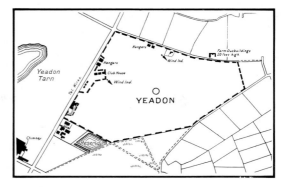

Below:
Leeds: Purpose-built luxury coaches are used to
carry passengers between the terminal building,
visible in the background, and aircraft parked on the
recently completed extension to the main parking
apron. The use of buses in such circumstances is an
economic alternative to the expensive option of
building fixed facilities such as piers and walkways
to connect distant parking stands with the main
terminal complex.   *Author*

Right:
Leeds/Bradford: A view of the northeast side of Leeds/Bradford airport taken in 1960. The white buildings in the foreground, including the hangar on the left, were erected in 1938 while the Avro hangar on the right was one of several built during the war to house aircraft from the shadow factory which is visible in the left background. In the foreground is a section of the then main runway (10/28) which was less than 1,100m long, too short for the operation of newer types of aircraft such as the Viscount, and consequently a brand new 1,650m runway (15/33) was laid down between 1963 and 1965. No sooner had this work been completed than the airport suffered a serious setback when the main terminal building was destroyed in a fire in May 1965 and the Avro hangar was pressed into service as an emergency terminal. Phoenix-like, a new modern terminal, incorporating a control tower, rose from the ashes and was opened in May 1968 although this development necessitated the demolition of the 1938 buildings. The Avro hangar was subsequently dismantled to make room for an eastward extension of the main apron. *Quadrant Picture Library 40532*

Left:
Leeds/Bradford: The current terminal building at Leeds with its distinctive control tower. Other improvements have included an extension of the main runway to its present 2,250m to allow the operation of modern jets. In 1983 the airport gained its own airline when Brown Air Services began operations with a turboprop Gulfstream I, but in 1987 they re-equipped with Shorts 360s and changed their name to Capital Airlines. By 1990 the company had expanded, its fleet including several BAe 146 jets, and a substantial route network centred on Leeds was established. Unfortunately, the airline ceased trading in 1990 causing a slump in passenger throughput from a peak of almost 900,000 in 1989/90 to just under 700,000 in 91/92. However, the airport, which recently celebrated its Diamond Jubilee, is confident that it is recovering from this blow and indeed it currently has several airlines flying a variety of scheduled services including British Midland, Air UK, and Aer Lingus, as well as a comprehensive selection of IT charter flights. *Author*

Below:

Leeds/Bradford: Plan of Leeds/Bradford airport showing its present layout. The extension of the main runway to the northeast in 1982/83 meant that a tunnel had to be built to carry the A658 beneath the new section. A short north-south runway, originally 01/19, has been closed for some time and is used only as a link taxiway. The dark block at the top of the plan is the old shadow factory which still stands. *CAA*

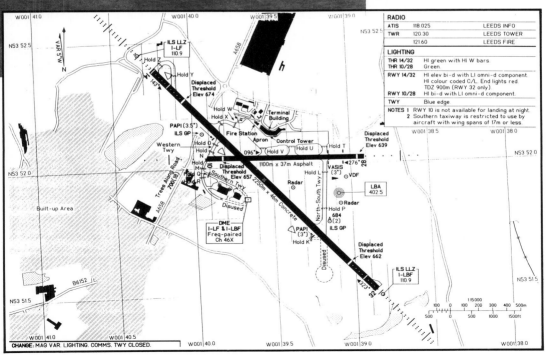

RADIO		
ATIS	118.025	LEEDS INFO
TWR	120.30	LEEDS TOWER
	121.60	LEEDS FIRE

LIGHTING	
THR 14/32	HI green with HI W bars.
THR 10/28	Green.
RWY 14/32	HI elev bi-d with LI omni-d component. HI colour coded C/L. End lights red. TDZ 900m (RWY 32 only).
RWY 10/28	HI bi-d with LI omni-d component.
TWY	Blue edge.
NOTES	1 RWY 10 is not available for landing at night. 2 Southern taxiway is restricted to use by aircraft with wing spans of 17m or less.

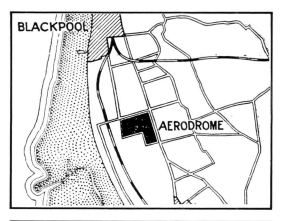

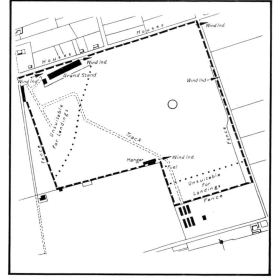

Right:
Blackpool: Squires Gate was requisitioned in 1938, even before the outbreak of hostilities, and during the war was used mainly as a training airfield by RAF Coastal Command, although Hurricanes and Defiants were also based here for a time. Blackpool attracted more than its fair share of attention from the Luftwaffe as it was the site of a massive shadow factory erected by the Ministry of Aircraft Production in 1939/40 for the building of Wellington bombers. A total of 3,841 were built here and the last was rolled out in October 1945 after which the factory closed down until reopened for the production of Hawker Hunters from 1951 until 1958 (374 built). During this time a new 2,000m runway was laid down to supplement the original wartime runways. Some of these features can be seen in this 1960s view of the airport taken from over the shallow waters of Morecambe Bay. The shadow factory is sited on the northeast corner of the airfield and the new main runway stands out well. *Aerofilms SV1828*

Above:
Blackpool: Blackpool's airport, Squires Gate, is associated with some of the earliest flying activities in the British Isles including the Daily Mail air meeting held in 1909. However, by 1911 the site had become a racecourse and during World War 1 it was used as a military hospital, providing convalescence for thousands of casualties from that conflict's bloody battles, and it continued as such until 1924. Subsequently Blackpool Corporation developed a municipal airport at Stanley Park, just to the west of the town but commercial services were started from Squires Gate by Blackpool and West Coast Air Services in 1933. In 1937 the decision was made to concentrate on development at Squires Gate and Stanley Park was eventually closed down. This drawing shows the airport as it was in 1935 with grass runways and the old racecourse grandstand serving as a combined clubhouse and passenger terminal. In fact this building remains in use today as the airport's administrative offices.

Left:
Blackpool: The Morecambe Bay gas and oilfield led to the natural choice of Blackpool airport as a base for helicopter support operations. The photo shows a party boarding an Aerospatiale Dauphin belonging to Bond Helicopters and such flights form an important part of the airport's activities today. In the background is the ATC building, based on the wartime watch tower. *Blackpool Airport*

Below left:
Blackpool: At the end of the war the airfield was taken over by the MTCA and was run by them until 1962 when it reverted to municipal ownership. During the immediate postwar years there were plans for a flying boat base in the Ribble estuary to complement a major trans-Atlantic airport at Squires Gate but in fact commercial traffic remained at relatively low levels, mainly consisting of various airlines serving the Isle of Man and Ireland. Current operators include Jersey European, Loganair and Manx Airlines, together with a modest programme of charter flights. However, the airport expects to attract over 300,000 passengers a year by the end of the century and to cope with this demand has plans for a new and long overdue terminal building together with an extension to the parking apron to allow nose-in parking by several Boeing 737 sized aircraft. Work on this project is due to start in 1993. *Blackpool Airport*

Ronaldsway (IOM): Ronaldsway has served as the aerial gateway to the Isle of Man since 1934 when Blackpool and West Coast Air Services acquired the land for use as an airport, although aviation activities had been recorded on the site as far back as 1929. During World War 2 the airfield was requisitioned by the Air Ministry and used as a base for an air gunnery school. In 1943 it was transferred to Admiralty control and was commissioned as HMS Urley. The Navy carried out extensive development including the laying down of no less than four hard runways with associated taxiways and hardstandings, together with an imposing three-storey control tower and other buildings. This busy airfield was used for a variety of basic and operational training purposes until the end of the war and the Navy pulled out in 1946 when it reverted to civil operations. Ronaldsway was purchased by the Isle of Man Government in 1948 since when it has been substantially developed and upgraded. However, when this photo was taken , in 1949, it still retained its wartime appearance and many of the wartime buildings remain. The substantial control tower can be seen and the apron is filled with some 20 aircraft including an Avro 19, three Airspeed Oxfords, a Miles Aerovan and several Dragons and Dragon Rapides. Almost certainly this was taken during that year's TT motorcycle races for which the island is famous. *Aerofilms A23429*

Top:

Ronaldsway (IOM): The modern airport terminal at Ronaldsway occupies the site of the hutted encampment by the airport entrance shown in the earlier photograph and the low building behind the ATP connects with the original control tower which is still in use. Shown here are the three aircraft types operated by the island's resident airline, Manx Airlines, who are unique in operating all three types of regional aircraft produced by British Aerospace — Jetstream, ATP and 146 (not shown). Formed in 1982, Manx is a member of the Airlines of Britain group and its operations contribute substantially to the half a million passengers a year currently passing though the airport. Apart from the terminal, other improvements have included the widening and lengthening of the main runway (09/27) in 1956/57 while the shorter 04/22 has also been lengthened. There is an amusing story told concerning the introduction of the quiet BAe 146 by Manx in 1987. Up to that date the main schedule to Heathrow was flown by a relatively noisy BAC-111 which departed at 7 o'clock in the morning but when it was replaced by the 146 the airline started receiving complaints from island residents who had used the 111 as a substitute for an alarm clock and were now oversleeping as the 146 did not wake them! *British Aerospace.*

Above:

Ronaldsway (IOM): The old RNAS control tower at Ronaldsway is still in use, the main alteration being the addition of a VCR cab on the roof. The other obvious feature is the aerial of the airport's AR.1 radar. In the foreground is an appropriately registered Shorts 360 belonging to Manx airlines. *Author*

Above:
Carlisle: The border town of Carlisle is served by the ex-RAF airfield at Crosby-on-Eden. Constructed in 1940-41, it was extended in 1942, but throughout the war served as a base for various OTUs and was abandoned in 1946. It was subsequently used on a limited basis by BEA who flew Rapide services to the Isle of Man and Belfast in 1946-47 but the few subsequent services to Carlisle operated from nearby RAF Silloth, leaving Crosby to deteriorate slowly. However, it was taken over by Carlisle Corporation in 1960 and run by Cumberland Air Services (Casair) who ran a flying club and provided a charter/air taxi service. Since then there have been attempts to provide the city with regular scheduled services and operators have included Autair, Dan Air, Air Ecosse and British Air Ferries. Most of these have been seasonal, typical destinations being the Isle of Man and the Channel Islands. In 1969 CSE took over the running of the airport and used it as a training base to complement their Oxford establishment. However, a slump in pilot recruitment caused the shutdown of this activity in 1980. Subsequently Specialist Flying Training moved in, flying the unusual NDN Firecracker and Gazelle helicopters to train foreign military pilots. However, this activity has also ceased although the airport continues in being as a busy general aviation facility. *Author*

Left:
Carlisle: An increasingly common sight at many airfields is a collection of vintage aircraft maintained and displayed by dedicated aviation enthusiasts. Carlisle boasts a selection of postwar British military jets including the Vampire, Lightning, Canberra, Meteor and Vulcan shown here. *Author*

Carlisle: Before the war, Carlisle's airport was at Kingstown, two miles north of the city. This grass airfield opened in 1933 and in fact was officially only the second municipal airport to be licensed by the Air Ministry. Facilities, as shown in this 1937 picture, were minimal and consisted of a small administrative building and hangar, and one large hangar. In the foreground is a petrol station which is of interest because it is laid out to serve cars at the front, while two more pumps stand at the rear to refuel aircraft! Only a few scheduled services were flown before the war and most of these were to the Isle of Man. During World War 2 the airfield was mostly used by No 15 EFTS flying Magisters and Tiger Moths. After the war it continued in use as an RAF training airfield until 1953 when it reverted to civil use. However, it was not capable of expansion and the airfield was closed down in 1957, the City Council eventually adopting the airfield at Crosby. *Quadrant Picture Library 14823*

Below:

Sunderland: Usworth, just to the west of the coastal town of Sunderland, was first used during World War 1 but closed after the Armistice and only reopened in 1930 as a base for No 607 (County of Durham) Squadron, RAuxAF, which initially flew Wapitis, but these were subsequently replaced by Demons, and eventually Gladiators in 1938. After 1940 the airfield was turned over to training duties and acted as home for various OTUs until flying virtually ceased in mid-1944. Significant flying activity started again in 1949 when it was used by No 23 RFS and other units until 1953 when it closed down again. It was not until 1963 that Sunderland Corporation took over the airfield and it then evolved into an extremely busy general aviation centre with two flying schools, and parachute and gliding clubs. In an effort to provide facilities for business charter flights, a small terminal and control tower (shown here) were built and at one stage radar was installed, although this never became operational. *Author*

Left:
Sunderland: Today virtually all trace of Sunderland Airport has disappeared beneath the enormous spread of the Nissan car factory. The airport was closed down in 1983 in order to provide land for the Nissan development which today is one of the largest employers in the northeast and is producing over 120,000 cars a year. The only significant structure of the old airport is the main hangar, which is the white building with the curved roof in front of the factory. This is of a particularly interesting Lamella design which originated in Germany and the first was erected at Heston, while Usworth's was the second. Other aviation interest is provided by the aircraft collection belonging to the North East Aircraft Museum which was originally housed on the airfield but was subsequently moved to its present site with assistance from Nissan. *Author*

Above:
Gamston/Retford: Situated on the A1 approximately 20 miles south of Doncaster, Gamston was a wartime bomber airfield built in 1942. Mostly used by RCAF squadrons of No 7 Group, the airfield reverted to a care and maintenance basis after the war and finally closed in 1957. Today the airfield is operated by A. F. Budge, an engineering company which has branched out into aviation activities and which has built a range of new hangars together with an administration block incorporating a control tower. Like many other ex-wartime airfields now finding a new lease of life, only sections of the original runways are in use — in this case some 1,200m of the original 1,800m R/W 03/21. One of the subsidiary runways is used for glider launching and there are two flying schools based at the field. Using experience gained in reopening Gamston, A. F. Budge were engaged in a project to build a new city airport for Sheffield and Rotherham, but the status of this development is now unclear as the company went into receivership at the end of 1992. *Author*

4.
South and
West

Bristol: Lulsgate opened as Bristol's airport in 1957 and has been progressively developed since that date. The original grass airfield opened in 1940 as a relief landing ground for Tiger Moths from nearby Weston-super-Mare but hard runways were laid down in 1941/42. After more use as a training airfield, it finally closed down as an RAF base in 1947 and was taken over by the Ministry of Civil Aviation. It was not until 1955 that Bristol Corporation purchased the site and started work on building a civil airport. The main runway was extended in 1963 to just over 2,000m. The airport was badly hit by the collapse of Court Line in 1974 and it was several years before passenger numbers returned to their former levels. This view shows the terminal complex with its roof-mounted control tower in the mid-1970s. In the background can be seen the A38 trunk road which provides convenient surface access to the airport. *Aerofilms 285079*

Above:
Bristol: Bristol's first municipal airport was at Whitchurch Down, a few miles south of the city. Officially opened in 1930 by the Bristol and Wessex Aeroplane Club, the airfield was taken over by the City Council in 1935 and by the outbreak of war in 1939 it had been considerably developed with a paved runway equipped with lighting , several hangars and a radio beacon. During the war Whitchurch became the main base for Imperial Airways and British Airways as their aircraft were evacuated from Croydon and Heston, while the ATA also established a major centre for the training of ferry pilots. By 1944 the two airlines had merged to form BOAC which moved its operations to Hurn in November of that year. After the war BOAC used Whitchurch for pilot training and various airlines flew domestic schedules. However, the airfield's location left no room for expansion and so the city opted to develop nearby Lulsgate as an alternative and Whitchurch subsequently closed in 1957. The photo shows Whitchurch in the mid 1930s, prior to the laying down of the runway and expansion of the hangarage facilities. *Bristol Airport*

Below:
Bristol: In recent years Bristol has seen considerable investment in passenger facilities. The terminal has been rebuilt and extended to give a doubling in size of the departure lounges and arrivals area. This work was completed in 1988 and officially inaugurated by HRH The Princess Royal. At the same time the Plymouth-based Brymon Airways was encouraged to start a hub and spoke operation based at Bristol using new DHC Dash 8s, one of which is seen taxi-ing on the apron. These aircraft connect Bristol with a variety of domestic destinations as well as Paris and the Channel Islands. Like most regional airports, there is a healthy IT charter programme and in 1991 almost 800,000 passengers passed though Bristol, a figure which is confidently expected to approach 2 million by the turn of the century. To cater for this traffic, a new terminal is planned which will be built on the north side of the apron in the area behind the aircraft in this picture. This should be open in 1994. *Author*

Southampton: Aviation activities on the grass alongside the Southampton-London railway line are recorded as early as 1910 but it was only in 1917 that the site was developed as a regular airfield when it was occupied by the US Navy as a depot for assembling and testing aircraft before they were dispatched to France. The hangars erected for this purpose are still standing, having been adapted for use as a terminal building. After World War 1 flying continued at the Eastleigh site but it was not until 1932 that the airfield was taken over by Southampton City Council and became a municipal airport. In 1936 Vickers Supermarine took over some of the hangars for assembly and testing of aircraft produced at their Woolston factory and it was in that year that the immortal Spitfire made its first flight on 5 March. During World War 2 the airfield was taken over by the Admiralty and was commissioned as HMS *Raven*. After 1945 the airport reverted to civil use and scheduled services were flown by various airlines, including BEA, to the Channel Islands and France. This 1964 photo shows the airfield almost unaltered from its wartime state, still served by grass runways. The sheds in the foreground belong to the Ford Motor company. *Aerofilms 128478*

Above:

Southampton: In 1961 the Ministry of Civil Aviation, who were then responsible for the operation of Southampton (Eastleigh), announced that they intended to withdraw facilities for commercial flying as they were not prepared to fund the construction of a sorely needed hard runway and associated taxiways. As airlines such as BUA and BEA introduced new turboprop aircraft (Heralds and Viscounts) they transferred their Channel Island services to Hurn airport near Bournemouth. However, the airport was purchased by Mr J. N. Somers, a well-known pilot and successful competitor in postwar Kings Cup air races, who provided the necessary finance to lay down a 5,500ft concrete runway which was completed in 1965 and, at the time, the airport was unique in being the only regional airport of any significance to be privately owned — the others all being government or municipally owned The result was a dramatic upsurge in the airport's fortunes as BUA, BEA and Cambrian Airways all moved back from Hurn and established a substantial network of scheduled services. This photo was taken in 1967 and shows a BUA Herald and Viscount, together with a Cambrian Viscount on the newly extended apron in front of the terminal building. Also visible are two BUA Mk 32 SuperFreighters which flew car ferry services to Cherbourg and the threshold of the new runway can just be seen at top right.
Aerofilms 175767

Left:

Southampton: Today Southampton is operated by Airports UK, a BAA subsidiary, and is served by a variety of airlines including Air UK, Aurigny, KLM Cityhopper and Air France. The traditional passenger and cargo traffic to the Channel Islands is still vitally important but in recent years considerable efforts have been made to increase services to European and other domestic destinations. Approximately 430,000 passengers are using the airport each year but Airports UK are planning to increase this to 1 million by the year 2005 by means of a £20 million investment scheme which would include a new terminal to replace the converted World War 1 hangars which can be seen behind this Air France ATR42. Behind the Aurigny Trislander is the modern control tower which replaced a small wooden structure precariously balanced on the apex of one of the cargo sheds. Southampton is one of the few airports in the UK to have its own railway station and the fast trains of Network SouthEast take just over an hour to reach London. *Airports UK*

Above:

Southampton Marine: Prior to World War 2 the problems associated with getting large heavily laden long-range aircraft into the air from airfields with finite runway lengths seemed to point to the flying boat as the only way forward. Both Britain and America developed such aircraft to institute scheduled services across the Atlantic and Pacific Oceans, and (for Britain) to serve the far flung parts of the Empire. Wartime development of such aircraft as the DC-4 and the Constellation, together with the construction of large airfields around the world meant that conventional landplanes eventually proved more practical. However, Britain persisted with flying boat development for a short period after the war and an outward sign of this was the opening, in 1948, of a new BOAC terminal at Berth 50 in Southampton Docks. The aircraft shown here at the official opening ceremony on 14 April was one of 12 Short Solents (a development of the Seaford which was originally the Sunderland Mk IV) ordered by BOAC in 1946 but their career at Southampton was short-lived as the airline terminated all flying boat services in November 1950. However, the independent Aquila Airways continued flying boat operations with Hythes and Sandringhams (also Sunderland developments) until 1959 when the terminal finally closed. *Quadrant Picture Library C90*

Hamble: The Solent area is rich in aviation history and one of the most historic sites was at Hamble on the eastern shores of Southampton Water. Confusingly there were three separate locations in the vicinity used for aeronautical purposes and these included Hamble Point, where Fairey maintained a seaplane and aircraft factory from 1915 until as late as 1948, while A. V. Roe built a new factory and airfield on the shoreline in 1916, but in 1926 the latter company opened a third and larger airfield a few hundred yards inland. This was known as Hamble (North) to distinguish it from the earlier Hamble (South) which contained the factory. Although land-based flying at the latter soon ceased, the factory was taken over by Armstrong Whitworth and was later absorbed into the Hawker Siddeley group. Among the many aircraft produced here was the Folland Midge and Gnat and today the factory is owned by Aerospace Structures, an independent company hived off from British Aerospace and specialising in the production of components for aircraft manufacturers around the world. Hamble (North) perhaps became best known as the site of the College of Air Training set up in 1960 to provide training for BEA and BOAC student pilots. British Airways eventually sold the College in 1982 when a glut of pilots made initial training unnecessary and the airfield closed in 1984. The photo was taken in 1970 and shows part of the College's fleet of training aircraft which included Chipmunks, Cherokees and Barons. Note the railway line which ran across the airfield to serve the Shell fuel oil storage depot built on the site of the old South airfield. *Aerofilms A205845*

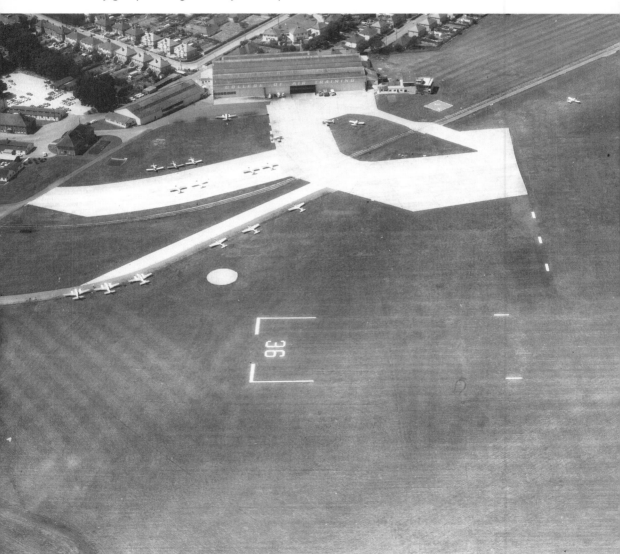

Above:
Bournemouth: Hurn airport is situated on the fringe of the New Forest just to the north of the seaside town of Bournemouth. It was originally built in 1941/42 and steadily expanded throughout the war, its operations reaching a climax on the eve of D-Day 1944 when it was home to no less than eight squadrons of Typhoons and Mosquitoes. However, after the invasion things quietened down quickly so that Hurn was handed over to the Ministry of Civil Aviation and became the main base for BOAC's international flights until 1946 when operations were gradually transferred to the new airport at Heathrow. In 1951 Vickers Armstrong took over some of the ex-BOAC hangars on the northwest side of the airfield and subsequently added further factory space enabling a production line to be set up. Initially Varsities were built here, but subsequently it became the main Viscount production centre and the photo shows the production line in 1953. The last Viscount was produced in 1964 but by then production of the BAC 1-11 was under way and this continued until 1982 after which the then British Aerospace factory closed down. *Quadrant Picture Library 29615*

Right:
Bournemouth: During the 1950s and 1960s Bournemouth was served by several airlines operating scheduled services to the Channel Islands, Paris and Cherbourg and these included Jersey Airlines, Silver City, BEA and Cambrian, but after

Southampton reopened with a new concrete runway in 1965, the services virtually disappeared overnight. Passengers fell from around 200,000 in 1965 to a mere 20,000 in 1967 and even today it has yet to regain the sort of traffic seen in the mid-1960s. In 1969 the airport was taken over by Bournemouth and Dorset councils and considerable efforts were made to attract new services, though with limited success. A new terminal, shown here behind a Belfast freighter belonging to Heavilift, was opened in the 1980s and caters for the modest number of passengers currently passing through.
John Greaves

of the airport is FR Aviation. who specialise in providing target facilities for British and NATO armed forces. Their fleet, which includes over twenty Falcon 20 jets, makes much use of the wartime dispersals on the north side of the airfield. *John Greaves*

Below:
Bournemouth: A plan of Bournemouth airport showing the two main runways and the multitude of parking bays and dispersals left over from the war. The civil airport facilities are in the southeast corner while the north side is occupied by several aviation companies including FR Aviation and Loveaux Engineering, as well as several flying schools. Despite the relatively low number of commercial transport flights, Bournemouth is one of the busiest airports in the country as far as aircraft movements are concerned and the cross runways and multitude of taxiways make ATC something of a nightmare. In this respect it is interesting to note that a resident of long standing is the CAA College of Air Traffic Control which, as well as training most British Controllers, also provides courses for student controllers from around the world. When the airport was owned by the MTCA, many student controllers first spoke to a live aircraft from the tower at Bournemouth but this is no longer thought necessary as most of the training is done on simulators. *CAA*

Above:
Bournemouth: The largest airline based at Bournemouth is currently the freight and parcels specialist Channel Express. Beginning operations in a small way during 1978 to provide a reliable means of transporting flowers from Guernsey to the mainland, the airline now has a fleet of nine Heralds and four Electras, which are employed on a Europe-wide network of cargo services. Another major user

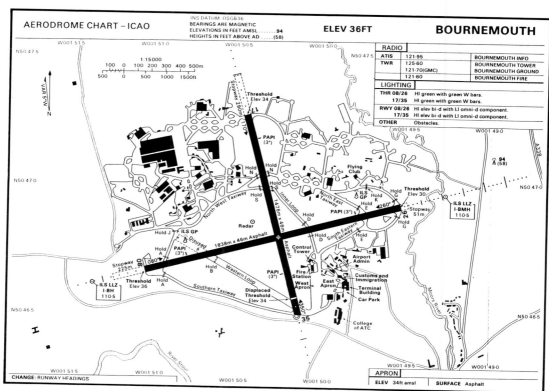

Portsmouth: Portsmouth was yet another air minded municipality which established its airport during the 1930s and this photograph shows participants gathered for the air display which formed part of the official opening ceremonies on 2 July 1932. Aircraft present include a fascinating contemporary cross section of military and civil types, including a Vickers Victoria transport and an Armstrong Whitworth Argosy II airliner — the two large biplanes in the foreground. Others included the Westland Pterodactyl, Bristol Bulldog, Hawker Fury, Fokker F.VIIA and Westland Wessex — the latter, parked in front of the hangar, belonging to Portsmouth, Southsea & Isle of Wight Aviation Ltd. In the years leading up to the war, Portsmouth was

a busy airfield with services being provided by International Airlines, Jersey Airlines and Provincial Airways as well as PS&IoW Aviation. However, the airfield also became important when the council successfully persuaded Nevil Shute's Airspeed Ltd to move into a new factory built at the corporation's expense in 1933 and sited in the open area shown in the bottom left hand corner of this photo. During the war the airfield was requisitioned and, amongst other tasks, was used for glider training. However, the Airspeed factory, taken over by de Havilland in 1940 and heavily damaged in an air raid that year, produced no less than 4,411 Oxfords as well as major sub assemblies of Horsa troop carrying gliders. *Quadrant Picture Library 11847*

Portsmouth: After the war Portsmouth quickly returned to normal and military flying ceased in 1946, although the airfield was not formally derequisitioned until 1949. Portsmouth Aviation, which had been established during the war from the former PS&IoW Aviation, started charter work and also carried out aircraft engineering and maintenance at their works centred around the original hangar and control tower. After producing a civil variant of the Oxford (Consul), the Airspeed factory concentrated building sub assemblies for Ambassadors, Vampires and Comets until it finally closed in 1960. In the meantime, several airlines were providing scheduled services and a new terminal and control tower were erected on the eastern boundary alongside the main A288 road leading out of Portsmouth along the shores of Langstone Harbour. The airport's proximity to water

had given rise to several projects for a major seaplane base to be established here but none of these ever came to fruition. The airport's fortunes suffered a major setback when not one, but two, HS 748s belonging to Channel Airways skidded off the grass surface on the same day after a heavy rain shower and crashed through the airfield boundaries. Fortunately nobody was seriously injured but subsequent restrictions by the CAA on the operation of public transport aircraft from grass airfields meant that the airport would have to lay a paved runway if it were to continue as a serious commercial venture. In the event the Corporation were reluctant to make the investment and the airport subsequently closed in 1973. This photo was taken in 1968 and shows the new terminal on the right by the road, while the former Airspeed factory is in the background at the end of the grass runway 18. *Aerofilms GF1608*

Above:

Portsmouth: As well as carrying out aircraft maintenance, Portsmouth Aviation also built and flew a prototype of their unique twin-boomed five-seater Aerocar and the sole example (G-AGTG) is shown at an air display in 1948. Production plans were abandoned in 1950 and this interesting aircraft was broken up. *Portsmouth Aviation*

Below:

Portsmouth: Since the airfield at Portsmouth closed in 1973, the land has been subject to continual development and is covered with housing, industrial premises and a large supermarket. However, there are still strong aviation links as both Hants & Sussex Aviation and Portsmouth Aviation are based here. The former has premises on the new industrial estate but Portsmouth Aviation, who concentrate on the production of ground support equipment for airlines, still occupy their original hangars, and the control tower, now a listed building, acts as a staff canteen. *Author*

Below:

Lympne/Ashford: Situated on the top of a ridge overlooking the flat Romney Marshes on the Kent coast, Lympne was once one of Britain's most important airfields as it offered a convenient point to start and end a crossing of the English Channel. Flying began here in 1916 and civil operations started in 1919. Between 1923 and 1926 a series of trials, sponsored by the Air Council and the SBAC, were held at Lympne to encourage the design of efficient light aircraft and the photo shows some of the entrants at the 1926 event. The monoplane on the left is a Bristol Type 91 while the line up on the right includes a Supermarine Sparrow II (furthest from the camera) and the Avro 562 Avis. In the 1930s Lympne was the departure point for several record breaking attempts by pioneering aviators such as Amy Johnson and Jim Mollison. An RAF presence was established in 1936 and the airfield was taken over by Fighter Command in 1939. *Quadrant Picture Library*

Left:
Lympne/Ashford: During the Battle of Britain Lympne was very heavily bombed and was temporarily abandoned due to extensive damage. Subsequently it was used as a forward operating base for operations against continental Europe. After the war it was taken over by the MTCA and it was from here that Silver City airways began their car ferry services, although these subsequently moved down the hill to Lydd. In 1955 the airfield was purchased by Skyways who built two large hangars on the hardstanding visible in this 1948 photo. The airline had ambitious plans which included the construction of hard runways and the operation of Stratocruisers on trans-Atlantic flights although this came to nothing in the end. However, Skyways started their successful coach-air services to Paris via Beauvais, originally with DC-3s, but later was the first airline to order the Avro 748 which entered service in 1962. In 1972, by which time a short runway had been laid down (in 1969 following an accident in which a 748 overturned on landing), Skyways were taken over by Dan Air who continued operations until 1974 when commercial operations ceased although some private flying continued spasmodically for the next few years.
Aerofilms 13661/48

Above:
Lydd: Although the RAF had flown from a temporary airfield at Lydd during World War 2, it was a different site that Silver City Airways selected in 1953 for the construction of a brand new airfield to serve their expanding car ferry services across the English Channel. Opened in 1954, Ferryfield was equipped with a passenger terminal, hangars and two tarmac runways — all built in the space of seven months! For many years the services prospered and this line up of the company's Mk 32 SuperFreighters makes an impressive sight around 1960. In 1962 Silver City became part of the British United Airlines Group and initially Ferryfield was as busy as ever but by 1970 the ageing Bristol Freighters could not compete with the modern cross-channel sea ferries and their last service, now under the colours of British Air Ferries, was flown in October of that year. Flights to Ostend using Carvairs continued for another year but after that the airport saw little commercial traffic until Dan Air Skyways flew their London-Paris coach-air service through Lydd from 1974 to 1979. The airport briefly closed in 1981-82 and since then has had mixed fortunes as various operators have tried commercial services. At present the airport is used mainly as a customs point for general aviation traffic routeing to the continent. *Quadrant Picture Library 37315*

Above:

Shoreham: Shoreham can fairly lay claim to being one of the oldest airports in the UK, having been established as long ago as 1911 and has been in continuous use ever since apart from a short break in 1922. The following year F. G. Miles started the Gnat Aero Company, although he flew from a site on the south side of the railway line which crosses the foreground in this picture. During the 1930s Brighton, Hove and Worthing formed a joint committee to oversee the development of a new municipal airport on the old site and an extremely attractive terminal and control tower, together with a pair of hangars, were built between 1934 and 1936 when this photograph was taken. The Southern Railway opened a nearby railway station and the airport was served by several Railway Air Services flights. In the early part of the war Shoreham was used by KLM, Sabena and DDL, instead of Croydon which had become a fighter base. After the fall of France, all civilian flying ceased and the airfield was used by a variety of operational units under the aegis of No 11 Group, Fighter Command. *Aerofilms R1616*

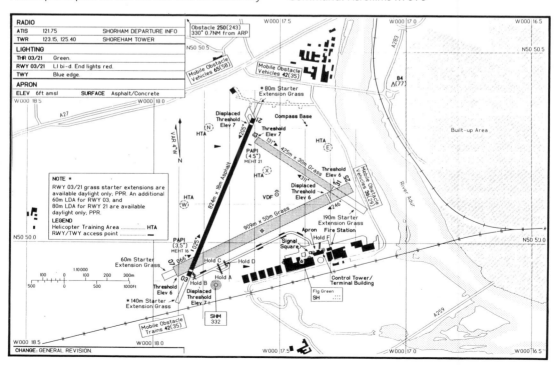

Below:

Goodwood: Goodwood airfield, near Chichester in Sussex, is a busy grass airfield with several flying schools and business operators based here. Originally earmarked as an emergency landing ground in 1938, it became a satellite airfield for nearby Tangmere and housed both RAF and USAAF fighter units throughout the war. A plaque near the present control tower commemorates the fact that the first American Fighter Group (31st) to be based in Europe during the war arrived here on 26 July 1942. The airfield was closed down in 1946 and from 1948 the wartime perimeter track was brought into use as a motor racing circuit and has been substantially upgraded for that purpose since then. In 1958 the airfield was reopened for private flying, a road tunnel under the racing track being constructed to provide access. The photo shows the recently constructed control tower set well forward of some of the seven available hangars from where a good view is obtained over the three grass runways. This has replaced a small temporary tower building which still stands although not visible in this view. *Author*

Left:

Shoreham: After the war Shoreham was taken over by the MCA until 1951 when it reverted to its earlier municipal status. F. G. Miles set up shop again and produced aircraft such as the Sparrowjet and the Miles Student, as well as carrying out overhauls and repairs on a variety of aircraft. The company became part of Beagle Aircraft Ltd in 1960. A new factory was built at Shoreham in 1962 and both the Beagle Pup and twin-engined B.206 were produced in quantity until 1970 when Beagle went into liquidation. In the meantime there had been a few cross-channel scheduled services flown by airlines such as Channel Airways and JFK Airlines but, in the main, Shoreham has remained an extremely busy general aviation airfield. One of its major problems has been poor drainage (being only two metres above sea level) and even the lightest rain can cause problems. However a narrow 824m tarmac runway was eventually laid down in 1981/82 and this has made life much easier. The 1930s terminal is retained and, indeed, has been carefully restored to some of its former glory. As such it is often used as a set in films depicting the 1930s — an episode of the popular Hercule Poirot TV series was filmed here. *CAA*

Above:

Goodwood: Goodwood must be the only airfield to boast no less than *three* control towers. Apart from the old and new towers located on the airfield itself, the former wartime watch tower still stands and has been converted into a restaurant and bar. It is now separated from the airfield proper by the motor racing track, a section of which can be seen in the foreground. Although no longer used for major competitions, the race track is used to train drivers and by various teams for development and trials. *Author*

Above:
Staverton: Yet another airfield with its origins in the 1930s, Staverton is jointly owned by Gloucester and Cheltenham councils. The site was purchased in 1934 and the airport officially opened on 18 November 1936, but by 1938 the RAF had moved in with No 31 ERTS flying Tiger Moths and Staverton was officially requisitioned in September 1939. Apart from the RAF training, the airfield was also used increasingly for test and development flying by a number of companies. Rotol Ltd, manufacturers of propellers, had already set up shop in May 1939 and they were joined by Folland Aircraft with their F43/37 engine test beds and Flight Refuelling Ltd. The airfield remained RAF property until 1950 although Rotol, now part of the Dowty group, remained in residence and were later joined by Smiths Aviation Division. During the 1950s the airfield was variously run by Cambrian Airways and Smiths, and it was not until 1962 that the original municipal owners took control again. In the 1960s Glosair was formed and at one time was assembling imported Victa Airtourers for sale in the UK. Also in the 1960s the Skyfame Museum was established here with the aim of preserving World War 2 aircraft in flying condition, a pioneering effort which represented the beginnings of the modern aircraft preservation movement. The photo shows the eastern side of the airfield in 1975 and the large aircraft in the centre is a Handley Page Hastings, which was once part of the Skyfame collection. Passenger facilities and air traffic control are housed in the small white building on the right and several new hangars have been added to complement the wartime structures. *Quadrant Picture Library*

Left:
Staverton: Today Staverton is an extremely busy general aviation centre with six flying clubs, several executive operators, aircraft restoration specialists and aircraft brokers and sales agents. Both Glosair and Skyfame have long since faded away but in their place are concerns such as Flight One which runs and maintains several interesting aircraft including the last airworthy Twin Pioneer. Airline traffic has remained spasmodic, although currently Brymon Airways and Air Corbierè provide links to the Channel Islands while there is talk of a local business starting flights to London City Airport. A modest investment programme has produced the new purpose built ATC and administration building shown here together with new taxiways and an improvement in passenger facilities. *Author*

Below:
Exeter: Commercial flying started from Exeter's airfield at Clyst Honiton in 1937 with services by Jersey Airways and Railway Air Services, although the official opening was not until 30 June 1938. With the outbreak of war the airfield was used by the newly formed National Air Communications and also by various detachments from Farnborough. By mid-1940 it was taken over by No 10 Group, Fighter Command, and Hurricanes of Nos 87, 213 and 610 Squadrons were based here during the Battle of Britain. In 1944 the airfield was used as a mounting base for American glider troops participating in the D-Day operations. After the War, Exeter was transferred to the MTCA in 1947 and for many years was the site of Chrislea Aircraft Ltd, who produced the unusual Super Ace and Skyjeep light aircraft. The aerial view was taken in 1973 and clearly shows the wartime runways and dispersals with the terminal area off to the left of the main runway. At this time the lengthened main runway had just been resurfaced prior to Devon County Council taking over the airfield in 1974.
Aerofilms 270385

Overleaf top right:
Exeter: Exeter airport had the proud distinction of being the last base for operational de Havilland Mosquitoes which, until the early 1960s, were a regular sight in the West Country skies. The aircraft belonged to No 3/4 Civil Anti-Aircraft Co-operation Unit (CAACU) and were used for target towing and radar calibration work. Most examples were TT Mk 35s, but this dual-control T Mk 3 (RR299) was used for pilot conversions and is shown at the 1960 Exeter Air Show. The CAACU was civilian manned and operated by Airwork Ltd under contract to the Air Ministry. After retirement, most of the Mosquitoes were purchased for use in the film *633 Squadron* and many subsequently passed into the hands of various museums and private owners. RR299 is still flying, having been carefully restored by British Aerospace at Chester. *Author*

Below right:

Exeter: Under the ownership of Devon County Council the airfield has seen a steady improvement of passenger facilities. This recent photo shows the modernised and extended terminal building surmounted by a new control tower, this work having been completed in 1981. It is interesting to compare this building with that at Ipswich as both were designed by the same architect and completed before the war although the latter's has not been altered or modernised. Exeter's main operator today is Jersey European who, in addition to flying scheduled services to various UK and European destinations, have had their administrative headquarters and engineering base at Exeter since 1986. The aircraft shown (G-JEAH) is one of eight F27 Friendships purchased from the Australian airline East West in 1990. Other scheduled flights are flown by Isles of Scilly Skybus and there is an extensive charter programme throughout the year including flights to Cyprus, Malta, Tenerife and Toronto. *Paul Morton*

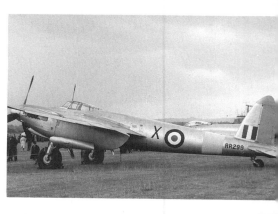

Below:

Exeter: Plan of Exeter Airport in 1992. The main runway (08/26) was further extended to its present 2,083m in the 1980s and is capable of handling Boeing 757s which are used on trans-Atlantic charter flights. The short cross runway (02/20) is disused. *CAA*

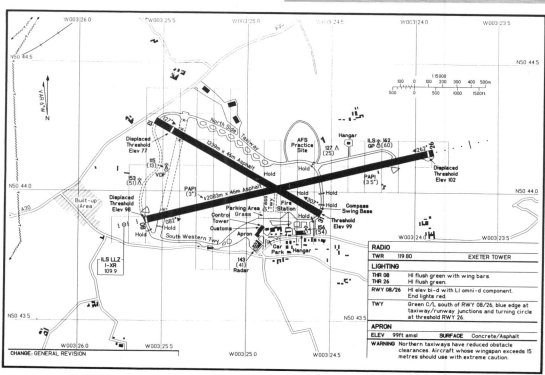

Below:

Plymouth: Plymouth's Roborough airport, five miles north of the city, has a history stretching back to 1923 when it was the base for pioneering scheduled flights to Birmingham, Manchester and Belfast. However, this operation failed and although private and club flying later started up, it was not until 1931 that the city corporation purchased the land and an airport was officially opened in 1931. The following year the Great Western Railway started air services to Cardiff and this, and other routes were subsequently operated by Railway Air Services. On the outbreak of war the airfield was requisitioned by the Admiralty but transferred to the Air Ministry in 1942. During the Battle of Britain, Gladiator biplane fighters were based here to help in the defence of the important naval base at Devonport. Unlike many requisitioned airfields, no hard runways were laid down and it remained as a grass airfield when handed back to the city in 1946. This photo was taken in 1965 and shows that no development had occurred since the war and facilities were limited to a single hangar and a clubhouse. Airlines such as Jersey Airlines and Dan Air using Rapides and Doves tried the occasional scheduled service which generally were unsuccessful. One resident airline was Mayflower Air Services which was based here from 1961, mainly serving the Isles of Scilly with Dragon Rapides, but this ceased flying in 1964 after one of the Rapides was written off in an accident at St Mary's.
Aerofilms 153198

Overleaf top:

Plymouth: Today Plymouth has been transformed out of all recognition with two paved runways, the longest (13/31) having a length of 1,170m, a new terminal building and control tower, and modern navigation aids including ILS. This has come about as a result of the activities of Brymon Airways which started operations from Plymouth in 1972 using an Islander for a network of West Country services. These were so successful that, in 1975, the airline took over the running of the airport from Airwork. It was in that year that the first tarmac runway (06/24) was laid down while the cross runway (13/31) was completed in 1980. From 1982 the airline began operating Dash 7 STOL airliners from Plymouth to Heathrow and since then its route network has expanded considerably. In 1987 runway 13/31 was extended to its present length and was equipped with an ILS system which greatly reduced the number of diversions due to bad weather. It was at Plymouth that Brymon proved the operating techniques now successfully incorporated into London's City Airport which has a runway of similar length. Despite Brymon's success at Plymouth, the airline is being hit by steadily increasing charges at Heathrow and Gatwick and has already dropped the Plymouth-Gatwick route for that reason. Although the airline, now merged with Birmingham European Airways to become Brymon European, retains maintenance facilities for its Dash 7 and Dash 8 aircraft at Plymouth, it has moved the centre of its operations to Bristol and the future of the Plymouth services is looking uncertain. *Author*

Right:
Plymouth: An unusual unit at Plymouth is the Britannia Royal Navy College Air Experience Flight which has been based here since 1960 for the benefit of trainee naval officers at nearby Dartmouth. The initial equipment was four Tiger Moths, the last in British military markings, and they survived until replaced by Chipmunks in 1966. One of the Tiger Moths (BB852/ex-G-ADPC) is shown here at Plymouth in the summer of 1960. *Author*

Below right:
Plymouth: In 1992 the BRNC Flight is still flying a de Havilland product — the Chipmunk T Mk 10 — three of which are shown lined up at Plymouth preparing for a training detail. In the background is the intersection of the two tarmac runways. Following a recent MoD decision, the operation of the BRNC Flight is to be put out to tender to private companies. The successful concern will have the option of purchasing the Chipmunks or introducing an entirely new type, likely candidates being the Slingsby Firefly and the Loveaux Sprint 160. *Author*

Bodmin: Bodmin in Cornwall is an example of a rare phenomena in the postwar British aviation scene — a new airfield opened on a greenfield site. Some four miles northeast of the town, it is easily reached on the A30 which passes close by. Facilities include a clubhouse, hangars and two grass runways, the longest of which offers a 610m take-off run. Home of the Cornwall Flying Club, it was also the birthplace of the Trago Mills SAH-1 which is seen flying over the airfield in 1986. Thought by many to be the finest British light aircraft of modern design, the SAH-1 first flew in 1983 but, despite its obvious qualities, it has not yet entered production. However, the rights to the design have now been purchased by FLS Aerospace at Bournemouth who plan to build an uprated version to be known as the Loveaux Sprint 160. *CAA*

Above:
Penzance Heliport (Eastern Green): When BEA were faced with the prospect of withdrawing their ancient Dragon Rapides from the Isles of Scilly service, they made the bold decision to institute a unique service using brand new Sikorsky S-61N helicopters which were delivered in 1964. Initial operations, staring in May of that year, were flown from the airfield at St Just, but by September scheduled services were transferred to a brand new, purpose-built, heliport situated on the coast just to the east of Penzance. Although not the first heliport in Europe, the company did claim that it was the first one to be fully self-supporting with terminal facilities for passengers and hangarage and maintenance support for the helicopters. This mid-1970s view of the heliport shows the helicopter landing square in front of the large hangar, with the passenger terminal just to the left. The railway line in the foreground skirts the sandy beaches of Mount's Bay to run into the British Rail terminus at Penzance. *British International Helicopters*

Below left:
Penzance Heliport: British European Airways Helicopters operated the S-61 out of the heliport until 1972 when it became British Airways Helicopters (BAH) following the merger of BEA and BOAC and by that time over 435,000 passengers had been carried. BAH maintained the service although demand for helicopters in the North Sea oilfields led to the brief substitution of an S-58T for periods in the late 1970s. However, by 1983 passenger traffic had risen enough to warrant the basing of a second S-61N at Penzance. A major change occurred in 1986 when British Airways sold off their helicopter operation to a company owned by the late Robert Maxwell and the name was changed to British International Helicopters. Despite the sensational collapse of the Maxwell Group in 1991 it is confidently expected that a new owner will be found to ensure the continued provision of the vital link to the Scillies. In the meantime BIH currently fly up to a dozen flights a day to St Mary's from Penzance, and also serve the island of Tresco. In addition, there are direct flights from Newquay (St Mawgan) to St Mary's and to date around 2 million passengers have used the helicopter services to the islands. Shown here in front of the hangar is G-BCEB, one of BIH's S-61N helicopters, which is permanently based at Penzance. *British International Helicopters*

Jersey: Situated some 80 miles from the British mainland, the Channel Islands were a natural base for early air transport services and Jersey was initially served by aircraft operating from the wide beaches of St Aubin's bay, adjacent to the island's capital, St Helier. However such an arrangement, dependent on the tides, could not cater for the increasing demand for reliable air services and so the present airport on the western side of the island was opened on 10 March 1937. The opening is recorded in this photo which shows one of Jersey Airlines' four-engined DH 86s parked by the impressive new terminal and control tower. This particular aircraft (G-ACZR, *La Saline Bay*) was delivered in 1935 and was later requisitioned and served with No 782 Naval Air Squadron until it crashed in 1940. Following the outbreak of war the airport was used briefly by the RAF before being taken over by the Luftwaffe after the fall of France, and it remained in enemy hands until the Channel Islands were liberated in May 1945. *Quadrant Picture Library 14005*

Top:
Jersey: After the war, commercial services were quick to start again and the airport reverted to the ownership of the States of Jersey. A 1,450m tarmac runway was laid down in 1951/52 and a substantial two-storey extension was added to the terminal building. Although BEA maintained a comprehensive route network, there were also substantial services by several independent airlines including Jersey Airlines, Cambrian, Channel Airways and, later, British United (CI). From the late 1950s turboprop airliners began to appear and the photo shows the arrival of Jersey Airlines' first Dart Herald in April 1961. The airline was the first to order the Dart Herald, in 1960, and the first of four was due to be delivered the following year. However, due to production delays, Handley Page made their prototype (G-APWA) seen here available for lease during that summer. In the background are DC-3s and a Heron belonging to Jersey Airlines, together with a BEA Viscount. By 1963, when Jersey Airlines became part of British United, the airport was handling almost 880,000 passengers a year.
Quadrant Picture Library 41670

Above:
Jersey: In 1980 British Airways drastically reduced its presence at Jersey allowing other airlines such as Dan Air and Air UK to operate an increasing array of services. In the meantime the terminal and ATC facilities have been enlarged and rebuilt to the extent that the original building has disappeared from view, although its structure is incorporated in the present building. In addition, a pier structure with additional departure lounges has been added on to the south side of the terminal. This Air UK Herald is shown on the apron in 1984 and represents a link with the the original Jersey Airlines through a rather complicated series of airline mergers and takeovers which have characterised the British airline industry since the war. Air UK was formed in 1980 from the merging of several companies including the original British Island Airways, itself an offshoot from British United (CI) which had taken over Jersey Airlines in 1962/63. Today the airline has services to several UK and European destinations flown by BAe.146 and Fokker 100s, and Jersey is one of Britain's busiest airports with around 2 million passengers a year. *Author*

Above:
Guernsey: Guernsey's airport at La Villiaze, in the southern half of this small but very popular island, was not opened until 1939 and enjoyed the briefest of careers before being occupied by German forces from 1940 until 1945. After the war it remained as a grass airfield until 1961 when a paved runway was finally laid down to permit the use of modern turboprops. Until then there had been severe problems in the winter when the airfield was often waterlogged and the author can remember a flight in a Jersey Airlines Heron from Guernsey to Paris in 1955 when the view from the window was obliterated by mud thrown up during the take-off! Since then traffic has steadily increased and a variety of airlines have maintained regular connections to the mainland including BEA, Jersey Airlines, Air UK, Guernsey Airlines and Air Europe Express. With the collapse of the latter in 1991, the rights to the

Gatwick route were taken over by City Flyer Express. The photo, taken in 1983, shows the modern control tower and operations block with one of Aurigny's Islanders in the foreground although these have now all been replaced by the larger Trislander. *Author*

Below:
Guernsey: A plan showing Guernsey's current layout with its single 1,463m east-west runway served by several taxiways. A modest terminal in the southeast corner caters for around a million passengers a year carried in over 70,000 flights. As a night curfew is strictly enforced between 2100 and 0615, this means that the airfield is extremely busy during the day, particularly at peak periods in the summer. *CAA*

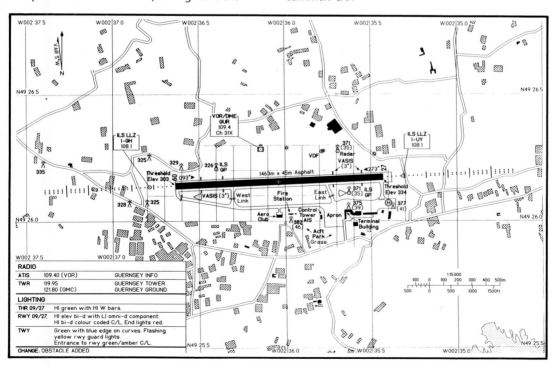

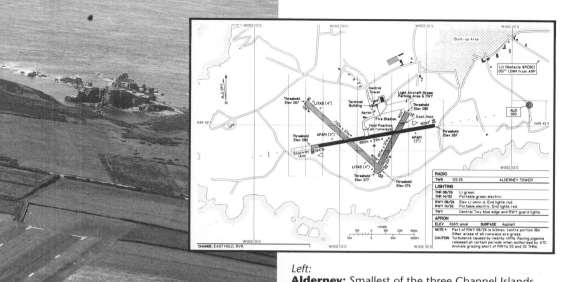

Left:

Alderney: Smallest of the three Channel Islands airports, Alderney is served almost exclusively by the Trislanders of Aurigny Air Services whose headquarters is here. The airport was opened as long ago as 1935, and claims to be the first operational airfield in the Channel Islands and the only one with more than one runway. Before the war it was served by Jersey Airlines using Dragon Rapides but was not used as an airfield when occupied by the German Army in World War 2. Scheduled services restarted by BEA in 1947 using Rapides which were later replaced by Herons. However, the massive state airline was keen to offload this relatively minor route and eventually the rights were taken over by the newly formed Aurigny in 1968 — starting a mutually beneficial relationship which continues to this day. The picture shows the airport in 1961 with the three grass runways clearly marked and the small terminal building just by the intersection of the two longest runways.
Aerofilms 93224

Above:

Alderney: An up to date plan of Alderney. The 880m main runway was tarmacked in 1968 to a width of 18m and was widened to 23m in 1990. A new terminal was built in 1967 and this is positioned much further back from the runway than the original facilities which have now been demolished. Finally a new control tower was erected in 1988. The number of passengers using the airport rose steadily from around 20,000 a year in 1960 to over 116,000 in 1990, although since then numbers have fallen off a little. *CAA*

5.
Scotland and Northern Ireland

Glasgow: Glasgow (Abbotsinch) is today Scotland's undisputed premier airport but it has had an interesting and chequered career. The city's original civil airport was at Renfrew, only a mile or so to the east of Abbotsinch, but by the mid-1960s this was becoming saturated and there was no room to extend the runways. Abbotsinch itself had opened as an RAF airfield in 1932 but from 1943 to 1963 it was run by the Royal Navy as HMS *Sanderling* and was then taken over by Glasgow Corporation for development as a major civil airport. The transfer from Renfrew was effected in May 1966 and this photo was taken shortly afterwards. The new concrete runways, taxiways and apron are clearly evident although the naval control tower remains in the centre of the airfield. An impressive new terminal building is served by two piers, the left hand for domestic flights and the right hand for international. Visible on the apron are a Heron, Herald and Vanguard belonging to BEA.
Aerofilms 163163

Above:

Glasgow: By the 1970 when this photo was taken, the airport was already expanding. Improvements visible include covered walkways for passengers boarding the aircraft which are parked nose-in, and an extension has been added to the end of the domestic pier. The Viscounts on the left of the picture show the new livery then being adopted by BEA, while the Vanguard taxi-ing in the background still carries the older red, white and black markings. At this time the airport was handling around 1.7 million passengers a year. *BAA*

Below:

Glasgow: Although Glasgow has developed steadily over the years, it received a major boost to its fortunes in 1990 when approval was given for trans-Atlantic flights to operate from here instead of Prestwick. This ended a situation which had been a problem ever since Abbotsinch opened and had grown to farcical proportions whereby the Boeing 757s of Air 2000 were taking-off from Glasgow with a full load, landing at nearby Prestwick, and then taking-off immediately for their true destination in America. The opening up of Glasgow as a trans-Atlantic gateway has led to a number of airlines, including Northwest shown here, flying scheduled services to the States while all the major British tour operators have flights to the popular destinations 'across the pond'. The British Midland aircraft in the picture are a reminder that British Airways do not have a monopoly on the lucrative Heathrow route, and it is indicative of the numbers of passengers using these services that Glasgow was the first British airport to be linked with London by an American-style shuttle service. This was started by British Airways in 1975. *BAA*

Above right:

Glasgow: Glasgow passed into BAA ownership in 1975 and today it handles over 4 million passengers a year, making it the fourth busiest in the UK behind Heathrow, Gatwick and Manchester. In recent years the Authority has invested £60 million in extending the terminal building to give 70% more space and the impressive new building, shown here, opened in the summer of 1992. A further £60 million is currently being spent on further developments including a new international pier, new taxiways and aircraft aprons, and a further terminal extension. This work is due to be completed by 1996 by which time the airport will be capable of handling up to 10 million passengers a year. *BAA*

Below:

Prestwick: In the pioneering days of postwar trans-Atlantic flying, Prestwick was a major gateway to the UK by virtue of its geographical position on the west coast of Scotland and because of its good record for clear weather. The airport was originally opened by Scottish Aviation in 1935 and until 1941, when the first runway was laid down, it was used mainly for RAF training. For the rest of the war it grew increasingly important as the eastern terminal of the Atlantic Ferry Organisation set up to arrange the delivery of American-built aircraft to the RAF, and by 1945 around 37,000 had followed this route. Following America's entry into the war in late 1941, the USAAF also used Prestwick as a major staging post. After the war military activity naturally declined significantly but in October 1945 the first postwar commercial trans-Atlantic flight landed at Prestwick which was taken over by the MTCA in 1946. Although used by BOAC, the airport was particularly popular with European airlines, which used the airport for a refuelling stop before setting out across the Atlantic. A typical example was this DC-6B of SAS at Prestwick in 1953. Note the control tower in the background, perched precariously on the roof of the converted hotel which served as the terminal building. *Quadrant Picture Library C515*

Left:

Prestwick: A 1960 view of Prestwick showing the old terminal and associated facilities. On the apron is a Boeing 707-420, the first of which had been delivered to BOAC the previous year. Unfortunately it was the development of long-range jets, such as the 707 and contemporary DC-8, which was to cause a significant decline in Prestwick's importance as they were soon capable of true intercontinental flights without the need for intermediate refuelling stops. Although the airport still had a major role as a diversion airfield and sustained limited services of its own as Scotland's international gateway, it was never to regain its standing as a front rank UK airport. *Quadrant Picture Library 40582*

Above:

Prestwick: An aerial view of Prestwick in the late 1980s looking southeast along the 2,987m main runway. In the foreground, to the right of the runway, is the modern terminal complex which was opened in 1964 when 225,000 passengers used the airport. On the left of the runway is the industrial complex, then occupied by Scottish Aviation Ltd, but now part of British Aerospace. Barely visible at top left is the military establishment which, until 1966, was the base for a substantial USAF presence, the last unit here being the HC-54D helicopters of the 67th ARRS. Since 1971 this has housed Sea Kings of No 819 NAS and the establishment is known as HMS *Gannet*. Until 1975 the airport was owned and operated by the Ministry of Aviation and its successors, but in 1975, in common with other Scottish Airports, it was transferred to the British Airports Authority. Despite continued investment and development, Prestwick's era as a significant passenger airport was effectively ended in 1990 following a decision by the Secretary of State for Transport that airlines would be free to provide intercontinental services from any of the major Scottish Airports, and would not be restricted to Prestwick as had previously been the case. In view of this ruling, the BAA relinquished its holding to a private company and the impressive terminal is now closed. *BAA*

Above right:

Prestwick: Despite the loss of passenger traffic, Prestwick still remains a busy airport. The British Aerospace factory produces the highly successful

Jetstream commuter aircraft here and the original 19-seater Series 31 has now been joined by the 29-seater Series 41, which first flew in 1991. Both aircraft are shown flying over the factory at Prestwick which will also become the production centre for the larger ATP, now renamed Jetstream 61. In addition, British Aerospace operate a highly successful Flying College, which trains pilots for airlines from all over the world using a fleet of Piper Seneca and AS202 Bravos. Other industrial concerns include Ryan Airline Services, the former British Caledonian aero engine maintenance facility established in 1980 which now has a world-wide customer base and provides work for over 800 staff. The Royal Navy helicopters remain and Prestwick is becoming an increasingly important centre for air cargo and is used, among others, by TNT and Federal Express. In fact the latter company has taken a 10% shareholding in the airport, a firm indication of its commitment to the future. *British Aerospace plc*

Below:

Edinburgh: Although Edinburgh is Scotland's capital city, it was slow to appreciate the benefits of air travel and it was not until 1947 that the first scheduled air service (to Northolt, flown by BEA Ju52s!) from Turnhouse was inaugurated. The airfield at Turnhouse originally opened as a military base in 1916 and at the outbreak of World War 2 was a Fighter Command station housing No 603 Squadron (RAuxAF) equipped with Spitfires. Although the airfield was handed over to the MTCA in 1947 for use as a civil airport, the RAF camp remained in being and No 603 remained operational with Vampires until 1957. In 1956 work began on a new terminal building and in 1961 the airport was closed while the main runway (13/31) was resurfaced and lengthened, civil operations being temporarily transferred to East Fortune (now closed) on the other side of the city. This view shows Turnhouse in 1971 with the civil terminal and apron in the left foreground with the RAF station and hangars beyond. The hangars on the right (south side of the airfield) belonged to the Ferranti company who had several aircraft based here for testing military airborne electronic equipment. The author was an air traffic controller here during the 1960s and well remembers the excitement caused when Ferranti's Buccaneer went flying during the test programme associated with development of the TSR-2, each time carrying 55min fuel for a flight planned to last 50min! *Aerofilms A214680*

Right:

Edinburgh: By the early 1970s Turnhouse was bursting at the seams with inadequate passenger facilities and a runway too short for the latest commercial jets. However, the city council was reluctant to spend the considerable sums of money required to develop the airport and consequently it was taken over by the BAA in 1971. An ambitious scheme was launched to construct a brand new terminal complex and a 2,560m runway (07/24) was laid down. The runway was completed in 1976 and the terminal was opened by HM The Queen in the following year. This photo, taken shortly afterwards, shows the view from the terminal across the parking apron to the new runway, which runs from right to left in the background. The Tridents of British Airways were the successors to the BEA Vanguards on the important Edinburgh-Heathrow route, which carried a substantial proportion of the passengers using the airport. *BAA*

Below:
Edinburgh: A recent aerial view of Edinburgh Airport showing the new terminal and runway. In effect, a completely new airport has been built immediately to the west of the original RAF airfield, the threshold of the old main runway being just visible at top right. By 1991 Edinburgh had risen to be the sixth busiest airport in the UK with almost 2.5 million passengers a year, compared to less than 700,000 in 1971 when it was the eighth busiest. The old terminal has now become a centre for cargo operations and a General Aviation Terminal has been built near the Ferranti site. Today the Heathrow route is flown by Boeing 757s in a shuttle operation, while Air UK provide services to Gatwick and Stansted and international airlines fly to a variety of European destinations. *BAA*

Below:
Aberdeen: Situated on the east coast of Scotland, over 100 miles from Edinburgh and almost 150 from Glasgow, Aberdeen was a natural target for operators of pioneering air services and the city's Dyce airport was established in 1934 as a base for Aberdeen Airways offering services to Wick, Thurso, Edinburgh, Orkney and Shetland. In 1937 the first international flights, to Stavanger in Norway, were started. During World War 2 the airfield was requisitioned and played an important part in the operations against German forces occupying Norway. Interestingly, it also served, between 1942 and 1944, as a base for flights between Britain and neutral Sweden by civil aircraft of Swedish Airlines. After the war Dyce gradually returned to civil use although a military presence was provided for some time by the Aberdeen UAS. In 1957 it was officially handed over to the MTCA and, in general, was a particularly quiet airfield served only by a few BEA domestic flights. This view shows Dyce from the north in 1971 when it still retained its wartime layout. A small terminal building and parking apron can be seen on the left (east side), while the wartime hangars and RAF camp are on the right. The author carried out part of his ATC training here in 1964 when an obligatory part of the practical training included visits to local whisky distilleries! *Aerofilms 214154*

Right:
Aberdeen: Aberdeen today bears no relationship at all to the sleepy hollow of the 1950s and 1960s. The factor which galvanised the airport, and the local economy, was the oil boom of the 1970s and this is best illustrated by looking at the passenger figures which rose from under 100,00 a year in 1968 to 1.2 million in 1978, 10 years later. No other UK airport has experienced such explosive growth and entirely new facilities have been built on the west side of the airfield to cope with this influx. The financial backing required to carry out this work was provided by the BAA which took over the airport in 1975 and invested over £10 million in two and half years. In the background of this picture can be seen the new terminal building (opened in 1977), while in the foreground are several new hangars housing the fleets of helicopters which now serve the numerous oil platforms in the north sea. The three original RAF hangars have been retained and a brand new control tower can also be seen. Apart from the main runway (17/35) the others are now used for parking aircraft or as helicopter pads. *BAA*

Right:
Aberdeen: The development of new facilities enabled the CAA, who provide ATC and technical services, to go to town on the design of a new control tower. The resulting 'ziggurat' structure is one of the most imposing of its type in the UK and opened in 1980. In the foreground is an S-61N helicopter of British Airways Helicopters which in 1986 was sold to the Maxwell Group and became British International Helicopters. Today BIH and Bristow Helicopters are the main providers of services to the oil rigs. *BAA*

Below right:
Aberdeen: Aberdeen's modern terminal currently caters for around 2 million passengers a year and is being refurbished by the BAA at a cost of £3.5 million. At the same time the airport handles around 100,000 aircraft movements a year, many of these being helicopters and the integration of intensive fixed and rotary wing flying activities calls for considerable skill on behalf of the busy air traffic control team. *Author*

Above:
Sumburgh: Sumburgh, situated on the southernmost peninsula of the wind-swept Shetland Islands, is amongst the most northerly of Britain's airports. Like Aberdeen, its fortunes have been dominated since the 1970s by the inexorable demands of the oil industry. Civil flying started here in 1933 but, as with many Scottish airfields, it was the impetus of war which led to development on a grand scale with three runways being laid down in 1941. As soon as the war ended the airfield was reduced to a care and maintenance basis until scheduled services recommenced in 1947. In 1966 the main runway (15/33) was extended to 1,426m to allow Viscount operations by BEA but there were still considerable operational problems due to crosswinds. Consequently, when oil-related traffic began to build up in the 1970s, the subsidiary runway 09/27 was lengthened to 1,180m in 1975, a task that involved considerable levelling of the surrounding area. To cater for the increasing passenger throughput, a new terminal complex and helicopter runway were opened in 1979. This photo shows Sumburgh at that time with the almost completed terminal in the background between the two runways. *CAA*

Right:
Sumburgh: A typical selection of aircraft on the apron in front of the terminal includes a BIH S-61N and a Super Puma belonging to Bristow Helicopters. In the background is a British Airways 748 and a British Air Ferries Viscount. The last 748s, affectionately known as 'Budgies', were retired by British Airways in 1992 and have been replaced by a total of 13 British Aerospace ATPs. BAF have been operating their Viscounts from Sumburgh since 1983 and are currently still going strong under contract to Shell Expro. However, the airport is not as busy as it was in the heady days of 1979 when passengers peaked at a yearly total of 620,000, having shot up from only 26,000 in 1969. Today approximately 300,000 passengers use the airport each year, the reduction being due to the fact that the advent of large long-range helicopters, such as the Chinook, means that many loads can now be flown directly from Aberdeen to oil fields in the Shetland Basin. *Malcolm Bradbury*

Below:
Sumburgh: An overview of Sumburgh from nearby Compass Head, taken in 1990, showing the terminal building and apron on the right while the control tower can just be discerned amongst the group of buildings on the left. In the background is the road leading to Lerwick, the island's capital, some 20 miles to the north although few passengers actually make the journey as most are in transit to and from the oil rigs. *Malcolm Bradbury*

Above:
Inverness: Prior to 1939, Inverness had been served by a small grass airfield on the banks of the Moray Firth, just a mile north of the city. However, a site at Dalcross, seven miles northeast, had been earmarked for possible use and this was taken over and developed by the RAF during World War 2 when it was used mostly as a training airfield. The MTCA took over the running of Dalcross in 1947 since when it has been used as a civil airport, although Oxfords of No 8 AFTS were based here during the 1951-53 period to train pilots during the Korean War. This view of the airfield was taken in 1961 and shows the unusual layout of the three runways which have a common point of intersection instead of the more common triangular layout of most wartime airfields. At this time services were operated to Edinburgh and London using DC-3s and Viscounts. Subsequent to this photo being taken, the two large VR hangars were demolished to make room for a car park and a modest terminal building. *Aerofilms A95883*

Left:
Inverness: A line up of British Airways aircraft at Inverness in the mid-1970s. The airport was closed for most of 1974 to allow the main runway to be lengthened from 1,660 to 1,887m in order to permit BAC-111 operations. The introduction of jets, together with the general increase in Scottish traffic due to the oil industry, led to an expansion of the terminal in 1979. In 1983 BA ceded the Heathrow route to Dan Air who built up a loyal following although BA have now regained the service following their takeover of Dan Air in 1992. Previously government owned, the airport is now owned and operated by Highlands and Islands Airports Ltd, a private company responsible for the running of many of the airports serving the more isolated Scottish communities. *CAA*

Dundee: Dundee's Riverside airport is one of Britain's newest airports, as it did not open until 1963. Previous aviation activity appears to have been restricted to a seaplane station just to the east of the city and used in both World Wars, although it was from Dundee that the Shorts Mercury/Mayo seaplane combination set off on 6 October 1938 on a flight to Cape Town during which it broke the world's absolute distance record. This event is commemorated in the naming of roads within the current airport which is sited on the north bank of the River Tay just to the west of the famous Tay railway bridge. The site was formerly occupied by playing fields and originally comprised a grass strip although the tarmac runway shown here was laid down in 1977/78 and lengthened to its present 1,100m in 1982 when a new hangar, terminal and cargo shed were also completed. Since its opening for commercial flying the airport has had mixed success in attempts to provide scheduled links for the city and many Scottish airlines including Strathair, Air Ecosse and Euroair have come and gone. However, there is a healthy general aviation community including Tayside Aviation who operate a busy flying school. *Aerofilms 603215*

Left:

Cumbernauld: Another Scottish airport developed in recent times is Cumbernauld, originally opened in 1966 as a grass strip to serve the New Town which began its development in the 1960s. For many years it was used only by private aircraft and gliders but in the late 1980s it was redeveloped with new purpose-built hangars, workshops and club facilities, together with an 820m paved runway. It reopened in 1989 and since then has become an important general aviation centre in Scotland. Owned by the Cumbernauld Development Corporation, the airfield is run by Cumbernauld Aircraft Services Ltd. and there are already plans for further expansion with a fourth hangar due to be erected in order to cope with an expected influx of private and business aircraft from nearby Glasgow airport due to commercial pressures at the latter. Given a clean sheet, the airport's architect has come up with a slightly unusual design for the buildings which are meant to vaguely represent an aircraft. The offices and control tower in the centre are the fuselage and cockpit, while the outstretched blue hangar facades represent the spreading wings! *Author*

Above:

Islay: The island community of Islay, off the Argyllshire coast, is served by the old wartime airfield at Port Ellen on the southern tip of the island. This was opened in 1940 and runways were laid down in 1942, although the airfield saw little operational use. Like many wartime airfields no longer required by the RAF or RN, Port Ellen was handed over to the MTCA in 1947 and since then has passed through the hands of various government departments and the CAA, but is now run by Highlands and Islands Airports Ltd. Since 1977 services have been operated by Loganair using Islanders and Twin Otters, one of the latter being lost while attempting an approach to Islay in bad weather during the 1980s. This photo dates from 1980 and shows the airport buildings clustered around the wartime control tower while a turning pan at the end of runway 08/26 serves as a parking apron. Since then the runway 04/22 has been withdrawn from use although the 1,545m runway 13/31, visible in the background, remains operational. *CAA*

Belfast Aldergrove: Situated some 15 miles northwest of Belfast City and adjacent to Lough Neagh, Aldergrove is currently Northern Ireland's premier airport and is one of the busiest in the UK and recorded at total of 2,170,173 passengers in the year 1991/92. Of these over 360,000 were international passengers with direct schedules being flown to Paris and Amsterdam by KLM and British Midland. Other international connections are offered via East Midlands and Birmingham (Brymon European) and there is a comprehensive IT programme which includes direct flights to the USA and Canada. Trans-Atlantic flights are no novelty to Aldergrove, as it was used in 1951 as the eastern terminal for record breaking flights by Canberra bombers which set times of 4hr 42min (westbound) and 4hr 19 min (eastbound) for the crossing. However, civil aviation in the province has had a chequered history and no less than four different sites have served as the city's airport since the first commercial services in 1922. Aldergrove itself was opened as a military airfield in 1918 and the south side of the airfield still houses a substantial RAF and Army establishment. The first civil passenger services were flown in 1933 by Midland & Scottish Air Ferries but from August 1934 all civil flying was transferred to Newtownards airfield, southeast of the city. Subsequently both Sydenham and Nutts Corner were used until 1963 when civil flying returned to Aldergrove following construction of a new terminal building and other facilities which were officially opened by HM The Queen Mother. Currently known as Belfast International Airport, it has been owned and operated since 1971 by Northern Ireland Airports Ltd, who have instigated a continuous programme of improvements including runway extensions, new taxiways, CAT III ILS equipment, terminal extensions and a new cargo centre. *P. McGuigan via Belfast International Airport*

Above:

Belfast Nutts Corner: In 1946 the former RAF airfield at Nutts Corner, approximately 10 miles west of Belfast, was taken over for use as the city's main civil airport. Originally built in 1941, the airfield was used by Coastal Command as a base for Liberators and Fortresses and in 1945 was transferred to the Fleet Air Arm when it was commissioned as HMS *Pintail*. It was returned to the RAF on 31 March 1946 and then became available for civil operations which continued until its closure in 1963 when Aldergrove reopened. This photo was taken in May 1961, and shows a typical collection of wartime RAF buildings, which are largely unaltered except for some additions to the station HQ in order to convert it to a passenger terminal. On the apron are a BEA Viscount and a Bristol Freighter belonging to BKS. The airport was served by a 6,000ft concrete runway (10/28) which was parallel to Aldergrove's runway some four miles away. After Nutts Corner closed down there were several occasions when aircraft supposedly inbound to Aldergrove would line up with the runway at Nutts Corner as, on a sunny day, the white concrete stood out like a sore thumb compared to the former's black tarmac runway! *Aerofilms A88613*

Below:

Belfast City: Many airlines flying UK domestic scheduled services see distinct advantages in flying to airfields situated close to the centre of cities and business communities. In this respect Belfast is fortunate in having an airport right on its doorstep. Owned by the aircraft manufacturer Shorts (now part of the Bombardier Group), Belfast Harbour Airport was made available for commercial flights in February 1983. At that time facilities were restricted to a few converted sheds in the southeast corner of the airfield but, by 1989, half a million passengers a year were passing through and a new terminal building was constructed to cope with this influx. At the same time the airport was renamed Belfast City Airport to reflect its growing status. Current operators include Brymon European, Gill Air, Jersey European, Loganair and Manx Airlines who fly scheduled services to a steadily increasing variety of mainland destinations and to the Channel Islands. In this picture a Loganair ATP taxies out towards Runway 04 and the new terminal complex can be seen on the right. *Belfast City Airport*

Top:

Belfast City: Sydenham airfield, now Belfast City, was built in 1936 by the Air Ministry and Shorts moved into new factory buildings in 1938. This photo shows the factory site on the west side of the airfield in 1943 with Stirling and Sunderlands awaiting delivery. After World War 2, all of Shorts remaining works on the Medway and at Rochester were gradually closed down and Belfast became the centre of its activities. Until very recently the company produced the popular Shorts 330 and 360 commuter aircraft at the factory and is currently completing an RAF contract for Tucano trainers. From 1943 until 1973, Sydenham was also a Fleet Air Arm base (HMS *Gadwall*) and, briefly, was used as a civil airport until Nutts Corner opened in 1946.
Shorts

Above:

Belfast City: An aerial view of Belfast City airport seen from an aircraft approaching R/W 04 from the southwest for landing. The Shorts factory is on the triangular spit of land to the left, adjacent to the cranes of the Harland & Wolff shipyard. Completed aircraft and major components are towed over the causeway to the flight test sheds on the left of the runway. The civil apron and passenger terminal are on the right where the airfield is bounded by the dual carriageway road from Belfast to Bangor. In the background are the sheltered waters of Belfast Lough. *Shorts*

6.
Government
and
Industry

Farnborough: Farnborough is synonymous with
the shop window air display currently held
biennially by the Society of British Aerospace
Constructors. The first SBAC Farnborough show was
held in 1948 and continued as an annual event until
1962 when the present biennial arrangement was
adopted in order to alternate with the Paris Air
Show held at Le Bourget. Up to 1966 only all-British
aircraft were allowed to participate and this 1956
view shows a typical gathering in the traditional
static park including such well-known types as the
Britannia, Viscount, Vulcan, Canberra and Beverley.
Star of the show in this year was the Fairey FD2
which had just captured the world's air speed
record with runs averaging 1,132 mph and two
examples can be seen just to the right of the
runway. Also in the picture is the prototype Handley
Page Herald in its original configuration powered by
four Alvis Leonides piston engines. Although
subsequently re-engined with two Rolls-Royce Dart
turboprops, it was too late to challenge the success
of the contemporary and similar Fokker Friendship.
In the background can be seen the control tower
and Farnborough's famous 'black sheds', where
much of Britain's pioneering aeronautical
engineering was carried out and this part of the
airfield remains much the same today.
Aerofilms A64938

139

Top:
Farnborough: The scene at Farnborough during the 1992 air show with hardly a British aircraft in sight. From 1966 onwards foreign aircraft with a substantial British involvement were permitted to be displayed under the 'sponsorship' of a British company. Thus, for example, the Dart-powered Fokker Friendship appeared in conjunction with Rolls-Royce. By the 1970s the increasingly international structure of the aerospace industry, plus the desire to increase the commercial appeal of the event, led to the present Farnborough International title and aircraft from all over the world now participate. The 1992 show was dominated by the Russian participation, exemplified by the Heavilift-operated Antonov An-124 which towers over the static park. In the foreground is a mock-up of the European Fighter Aircraft displayed by British Aerospace who have recently moved their corporate headquarters to Farnborough on a permanent basis. Behind the Antonov are the famous black sheds, now owned by the Defence Research Agency, which has replaced the Royal Aircraft Establishment. For the future Farnborough is being actively marketed as a business airport for London and an executive terminal is run by Carroll Aircraft Corporation.
Author

Above:
Radlett: Before moving to Farnborough, the postwar SBAC shows in 1946 and 1947 were held at Handley Page's Radlett aerodrome just north of London and this photo shows the line up at the second of these events. This was an exciting time for the aircraft industry and there was an interesting mix of aircraft taking part including jets such as the de Havilland DH 108 which subsequently became the first British aircraft to exceed the speed of sound. The row of aircraft on the right of this picture includes several new British airliners including the Avro Tudor, Airspeed Ambassador and the Handley Page Hermes. Handley Page had built their reputation on the construction of large aircraft and fiercely resisted attempts in the 1960s to force them into the rationalisation of Britain's aircraft industry when many other famous names were absorbed into larger groupings. Ultimately this led to the company's downfall and the airfield closed in 1970 when production ceased after 51 years.
Aerofilms A4922

Above:

Hatfield: The de Havilland company moved from their original premises at Stag Lane to Hatfield in 1930, although the earlier airfield remained open until 1934 and thereafter was the site of the company's engine division. However, Hatfield was the home to many of the most famous de Havilland aircraft including the Tiger Moth, Dragon Rapide, Albatross, and Mosquito. De Havillands were early pioneers in the jet age, building their own engines and the highly successful family of Vampire/Venom jet fighters. The first British aircraft to exceed the speed of sound, the DH 108, was built here but Hatfield's most famous product must surely be the graceful Comet — the world's first jet airliner. The tragic crashes which followed the Comet's entry into service were part of the sad price the company had to pay for being the first in a previously untried field, but the lessons learnt were applied not only to the later Comets but to almost all the world's first and second generation jet airliners. Seen here is the prototype Comet 4 (G-APDA) being rolled out in front of the control tower and main hangar at Hatfield prior to its first flight in 1958. *BAe/Winged Memories*

Below:

Hatfield: In 1992 British Aerospace, successors to de Havilland and Hawker Siddeley, announced that aircraft production will cease at Hatfield and the remaining BAe 146 production will be moved to Woodford. At the moment there are no plans actually to close the airfield where BAe maintains London Business Aviation Ltd to operate and run an executive jet centre on the airfield. This popular facility for business aircraft visiting the capital is shown in the photograph. Although nothing formal has been said, there remains a remote possibility that production of the Corporate Jets 1000 (née DH 125) may be brought here from Chester in order to free space required for Airbus wing production. It would be fitting if this best selling old de Havilland design should return to its birthplace, but at the moment such a happy outcome seems unlikely. *BAe/Winged Memories*

Cranfield: Cranfield was one of several RAF airfields built in the late 1930s as part of the prewar Expansion scheme. In fact Cranfield was one of the first to be laid down, in 1935, and it opened in 1937. It was also one of the first to have paved runways and by 1945 had two 1,830m runways and one of 1,000m. Today the airfield is home to the campus of the Cranfield Institute of Technology (CIT) which acts as a university to Britain's aviation and air transport industries, running courses on everything from engineering to airline management. It is also home to the International Test Pilots School, a civilian organisation which was founded in 1985 and has performed a number of actual test programmes on aircraft such as the PC-6, Tucano and Chichester Miles Leopard as well as training military and civilian test pilots from around the world. During the 1980s Cranfield was the venue for the popular PFA rally (now held at Wroughton) and this photo was taken as the airfield prepared for the 1984 event. The former RAF station and its collection of imposing Expansion period Type C hangars, on the right of the photo, are now used as the CIT campus. *Aerofilms 452076*

Rearsby: Rearsby, near Leicester, was the home of Auster Aircraft from 1946 until taken over by Beagle Aircraft in 1961. In fact the association with Auster went back to 1938 when Taylorcraft Aeroplanes (England) was formed to produce the Taylorcraft C two-seater high-wing monoplane under licence from the American company. The aircraft were built at Thurmaston and then taken three miles by road to Rearsby, home of the County Flying Club, for final assembly and testing. During the war several hundred developed versions, known as Austers, were built for the RAF and Army, and in 1946 the company changed its name to Auster Aircraft and moved all production facilities to Rearsby. For the next 15 years the company was a major force in British light aircraft industry and the various Austers, Autocrats, Aiglets, Arrows and Autocars still fly today in considerable numbers. In 1961 the company was taken over by the Pressed Steel Group, which also took over F. G. Miles at Shoreham with the intention of building a strong force in the world manufacture of light aircraft. The new company was designated Beagle Auster Aircraft Ltd, and the initial products at Rearsby were rebuilt ex-Army AOP.6 aircraft which were sold as the Beagle Terrier and the tricycle-undercarriaged four-seater Airedale which first flew in April 1961. The Auster name was finally dropped in 1962 when Beagle aircraft opened a new factory at Shoreham to produce the all-metal Pup trainer. However, production of the Airedale (43 built) and the Terrier conversions continued until the mid-1960s when Rearsby finally closed. The 1962 photo shows the Beagle Auster name on the hangar roof and there are several AOP.6 aircraft parked nearby awaiting conversion while the prototype Airedale is just visible beside the rear right hand hangar. *Aerofilms 102218*

Above:
Dunsfold: Owned and operated by British Aerospace (Military Aircraft), Dunsfold is the production centre for the versatile Harrier/Sea Harrier and AV-8 STVOL fighter, and the latest GR7 variant, jointly produced with McDonnell Douglas, is shown flying over the BAe factory and flight test sheds. The site was not developed as an airfield until 1942 and was used mainly by Mitchell bombers of Nos 98,180,226 and 320 Squadrons, RAF, until towards the end of 1944 when operations were transferred to continental bases. During 1945 it was used as a staging base by RAF Dakotas flying repatriated PoWs back to Britain. The following year it was leased by the independent airline Skyways for use as their main base until they went into liquidation in 1950. However, it was in that year that Dunsfold started its association with the aircraft manufacturing industry when Hawker Aircraft moved in and set up a final assembly and flight test facility using the wartime hangars. Originally Seahawks and Hunters were flown here, including the red painted WB188 which gained the World Air Speed Record in 1953, and more recently Hawks and Harriers. Dunsfold is virtually the home of the Harrier as the original P1127 made its first hovering flights here in 1960 and has been followed by the Kestrel, Harrier, Sea Harrier and AV-8A/B. *British Aerospace (Military Aircraft) plc*

Left:
Dunsfold: Inside the control tower at Dunsfold in 1952. As one of the country's foremost centres for high speed flying, the airfield was given the latest equipment. This control console, although looking dated to modern eyes, had just been built and installed by the Marconi company and the controller is flanked by the circular dials of their AD200F automatic direction finding equipment which could give extremely rapid and accurate bearings from the radio transmissions of aircraft. The author remembers using identical equipment at Ashford as late as 1974. *Quadrant Picture Library*

Hawarden: The British Aerospace factory at Hawarden, near Chester, was originally built in 1937-39 as a shadow factory for the production of Vickers Wellington bombers, over 5,500 being built up to 1945. The airfield itself was already in use as a relief landing ground for nearby RAF Sealand and during the war it was used by various OCUs, as a centre of the Air Transport Auxiliary (ATA), and by No 48MU as an aircraft storage centre. By the end of the war Vickers were also producing Lancasters but aircraft production ceased in 1945, the factory being used for the manufacture of prefabricated houses (the famous 'prefabs') until 1948 when it was taken over by de Havilland and subsequently a wide range of aircraft including Doves, Herons, Vampires, Venoms, Hornets, Mosquitoes and Comet 4s were built here. This photograph shows Hawarden during those golden days with a line up of Vampires Venoms, Doves and Chipmunks outside the flight test hangar in the early 1950s. *BAe/Winged Memories*

Left:
Hawarden: In the 1960s Hawarden became the sole centre for production of the DH 125 executive jet , still in production today although known as the Corporate Jets 1000. However, the airfield is now home to British Aerospace Airbus Ltd who occupy the massively extended production facility shown in the centre of this recent picture. The company produces wings for all Airbus variants and celebrated the delivery of the 1,000th set in early 1992. Total length of the production line is just over 1.3 miles, one of the longest in Europe, and completed wing sets are shipped out by road to Manchester or Filton for air delivery to Toulouse. However, plans are being considered to extend Hawarden's short 1,437m runway to accommodate larger aircraft so that wingsets can be delivered direct by air. BAe125/1000 airframes are also built here, but are then towed across to the Corporate Jets hangars on the far side of the airfield for completion and fitting out to customers' requirements. *British Aerospace Airbus Ltd*

Below:
Hawarden: The imposing control tower at Hawarden is adapted from the original wartime building and stands on the west side of the airfield, away from the factory. In addition to flying connected with the de Havilland/BAe factory, efforts have been made to encourage commercial flying and, over the years, a few airlines have operated from Hawarden including Liverpool-based Starways and their successor, British Eagle, while Air Wales briefly flew a Chester-Cardiff service. *Author*

Above left:
Woodford: Woodford is situated a few miles to the southeast of Manchester and is today a major British Aerospace production and flight testing centre. It was originally opened in 1924 under the ownership of A. V. Roe and over the years the full range of Avro aircraft have been built and flown here, from the Avian and 504 through to the last types to bear the name of this famous marque, the Vulcan bomber and the 748 airliner. The main factory buildings grew up on the north side of the airfield while the flight test department was housed in separate buildings and hangars on the south side, the latter being shown here shortly before the outbreak of World War 2. Lined up on the grass are several Ansons (11,020 being built between 1936 and 1952) but the aircraft nearest the hangars is a Blenheim, one of a total of 1,000 built by Avro under a Bristol sub-contract. The most famous product to appear on the Woodford production lines was the Lancaster which first flew in October 1941, although only just over half the 7,374 built were actually produced by Avro, the remainder being sub-contracted to other manufacturers. *British Aerospace Manchester*

Left:
Woodford: Avro Vulcans on the Woodford production lines 1957. These early B Mk 1s were left in a natural all-metal finish, but shortly afterwards all Vulcans were given the all-white anti-radiation finish which characterised the V-Bombers in the 1960s. The aircraft on the right (XA896) was one of the first to be delivered to the RAF, going to No 230 OCU early in 1957. *British Aerospace Manchester*

Above:
Woodford: A view of Woodford today showing the British Aerospace factory in the foreground with the flight test sheds in the background on the other side of the airfield. In a recent reorganisation of BAe production facilities, manufacture of the ATP airliner will be moved to Prestwick and, with Hatfield closing, Woodford will be the sole production line for the BAe 146 RJ series and the airfield will be the main flight testing centre for all the company's civil aircraft programmes. The airfield has a 2,292m main runway (07/25) although a displaced threshold currently restricts the landing distance on runway 25 to 1,671m. A link with the past is maintained with one of the last potentially airworthy Vulcans being retained by British Aerospace and it can be seen parked on a dispersal by the right hand end of the factory. *British Aerospace Manchester*

Filton: Filton airfield, north of Bristol, has been a centre of aircraft manufacture since 1910 when the Bristol and Colonial Aeroplane Co set up shop in premises leased from the Bristol Tramways Co. During World War 1 the Bristol company expanded considerably and the airfield was also used by the RFC. In the interwar period production facilities were maintained in being during the lean 1920s but the rearmament programme in the 1930s brought an enormous expansion in factory facilities and staff numbers. By 1939 there were factories covering over 2.5 million sq ft of floor space while the works and airfield occupied over 700 acres. Runways were laid down in 1941/42 but a further significant expansion took place in 1946 in preparation for Britain's new giant airliner — the Bristol Brabazon. This 100-seater eight-engined aircraft was expected to cruise at up to 325 mph over a range of 5,500 miles. Serious design work started in 1944 and the prototype flew in September 1949. In the meantime a massive new assembly hangar, shown here, was built and the runway extended to a total length of 2,450m, involving the diversion of the main A38 road and the partial demolition of the village of Charlton. This photo was taken prior to the Brabazon's first flight and the prototype can be seen on the right with the wing access panels to the eight Centaurus piston engines in the open position. A BOAC Constellation at the other end of the apron gives some scale, although the Brabazon's dimensions were slightly less than one of today's 747s and its maximum weight was less than half. The prototype and another partially complete aircraft were scrapped in 1953 but the flight sheds remain, having been used for production of the Britannia and today house a substantial overhaul and repair maintenance facility run by British Aerospace, the current airport owners.
Aerofilms 23246

Yeovil: The airfield at Yeovil in Somerset is the base of Westland Helicopters and first opened in 1917 since when it has an unbroken history as an aircraft production centre. Founded in the closing stages of World War 1, initially to build aircraft for other manufacturers, Westland branched out on their own in 1919 with the first of their own designs — the four-seater single-engined Limousine. Subsequently the company produced a number of successful aircraft up to 1939 including the Wapiti, Wallace and Lysander, as well as the three-engined Wessex, which helped to pioneer many domestic air routes in the 1930s. This photo shows the factory complex in the southeast corner of the airfield around 1930 with a Wessex and another aircraft parked in front of the hangars. Note the London & South Western Railway branch line from Yeovil Town to Taunton running alongside the airfield boundary. *Westland Helicopters*

151

Yeovil: An up to date view of Yeovil showing how the factory complex has expanded to become the largest helicopter manufacturing facility in Europe. Westland's last fixed wing aircraft to be produced was the turboprop Wyvern naval strike aircraft which became operational in 1953. In the meantime the company had already begun to concentrate on helicopter production following an agreement with the American Sikorsky company for the licence production of the S-51 and subsequent designs. Today Westland is actually owned by Sikorsky following a takeover in 1986 but retains its name and has autonomous design and production facilities. Helicopters, of course, do not need tarmac runways and consequently the grass airfield has remained virtually unchanged except where factory expansion has encroached. The black-roofed sheds fronting on to the airfield in the earlier picture can now be seen behind the white-roofed main assembly building and other buildings and car parks have spilled over the now closed railway line. *Westland Helicopters*

Bembridge: Bembridge, a pleasantly situated airport on the Isle of Wight, is the home of Pilatus-Brittan-Norman (PBN), producers of the highly successful Islander twin engined utility aircraft which first flew in 1965. Since then over 1,200 have been built including approximately 75 of the three-engined BN-2/3 Trislander variant. Since 1969 Islander airframes have been built in Romania, Belgium and the Philippines and are flown to the Bembridge factory for fitting out and completion. All sales and customer support is also based at Bembridge. Brittan Norman was taken over by Pilatus Aircraft Ltd of Switzerland, itself a member of the Oerlikon-Bührle Group, in 1979 and since then a considerable investment has been made in the factory and airfield facilities. This photo shows the expanded production sheds and a new terminal building and control tower complex which has replaced an old wooden building on the south side of the airfield. *PBN*

Left:
Bembridge: Investment from Pilatus enabled construction of a much needed 837 m concrete runway (12/30) to go ahead in 1979/80. This allowed intensive Islander test and demonstration flying to continue on a year round basis; previous winter operations had been hampered by the low lying airfield's tendency to become waterlogged. The taxiway linking the PBN factory on the east side of the airfield with the mid point of the runway was originally laid down as a starter strip in the 1970s in an early attempt to improve facilities. This was long enough for Islanders to attain flying speed before they ran on to the grass areas. *PBN*

Bembridge: Bembridge airfield in 1962 showing the original grass airfield before the Brittan Norman factory was erected and the hard runway laid down. At this time the airfield was little changed from prewar days and the original hangar (erected 1935) and clubhouse, can be seen beside the public road on the southern boundary. There has been an airfield on this site since World War 1 and apart from the PBN involvement it has catered mostly for private flying. However, there were several attempts to operate scheduled services to the mainland including Spartan Airways and Channel Air Ferries in the 1930s and a short-lived car ferry service in the 1950s from Southampton by Silver City Airways using Bristol Freighters. *Aerofilms A102896*

APPENDIX I.

AIRPORT IDENTIFICATION CODES

Communications play an important role in commercial aviation and, as well as the use of radio for ATC purposes, there are two separate teleprinter networks which link the world's airports. The first of these is the Aeronautical Fixed Telecommunications Network (AFTN) which has been established mainly for ATC purposes and is used for sending flight plans and other operational messages, as well as weather reports and forecasts, and other information useful to aircraft operators. For the sake of brevity and for addressing purposes, the International Civil Aviation Organisation (ICAO) has allocated each airport a four letter identifying code, known as a Location Indicator, which consists of a four letter code group. In this system the first letter indicates the part of the world, the second the country, the third the region or area within a country, and the last letter denotes a specific airport. A typical example: Edinburgh (Code EGPH) where E = Northern Europe, G = United Kingdom, P = Scottish region, H = Turnhouse.

Over the years the airlines have established their own network, Sita, which is used mainly for passing commercial messages such as passenger loads, departure times , and fuel requirements. Under this system each airport has its own discrete three letter code and this will be seen, for example, on tags affixed to passengers' luggage to ensure that it is sent to the correct destination. In many cases these codes are self evident such as LHR for London Heathrow. In the United States the two systems are uniquely combined so that the ICAO code for an airfield is the same as the Sita code with the letter K (=United States) added as a prefix. Thus Miami has an ICAO code of KMIA while its Sita code is MIA.

These codes are a convenient form of shorthand which many enthusiasts now use for their own purposes. The following text is a list of identifying codes applicable to the airports and airfields that are described in this book.

Airport	ICAO Code	Sita	Notes
ABERDEEN — DYCE	EGPD	ABZ	
ALDERNEY	EGJA	ACI	
BATTERSEA HELIPORT	EGLW		
BELFAST — NUTTS CORNER			Closed 1963
BELFAST — ALDERGROVE	EGAA	BFS	
BELFAST CITY — SYDENHAM	EGAC	BHD	
BEMBRIDGE	EGHJ		
BIGGIN HILL	EGKB	BGN	
BIRMINGHAM — ELMDON	EGBB	BHX	
BLACKBUSHE	EGLK		
BLACKPOOL	EGNH	BLK	
BODMIN	EGLA		
BOURNEMOUTH — HURN	EGHH	BOH	
BRISTOL — FILTON	EGTF	FLO	
BRISTOL — LULSGATE	EGGD	BRS	
CARDIFF WALES — RHOOSE	EGFF	CWL	
CARLISLE — CROSBY-ON-EDEN	EGNC	CAX	
CHICHESTER — GOODWOOD	EGHR		
COVENTRY — BAGINTON	EGBE	CVT	
CRANFIELD	EGTC		
CROYDON			Closed 1959
CUMBERNAULD	EGPG		
DENHAM	EGLD		
DERBY — BURNASTON			Closed
DUNDEE — RIVERSIDE	EGPN	DND	
DUNSFOLD	EGTD		

Southampton Airport has been a natural base for flights to the Channel Islands since the beginning of commercial air services. The Trilanders belonging to Aurigny are the only aircraft flying directly to Alderney from the mainland but several airlines fly to both Jersey and Guernsey. *Airports UK Ltd*

Airport	ICAO Code	Sita	Notes
EAST MIDLANDS — CASTLE DONINGTON	EGNX	EMA	
EDINBURGH — TURNHOUSE	EGPH	EDI	
ELSTREE	EGTR		
EXETER	EGTE	EXT	
FAIROAKS	EGTF		
FARNBOROUGH	EGUF/EGLF		
GAMSTON/RETFORD	EGNE		
GLASGOW — ABBOTSINCH	EGPF	GLA	
GLOUCESTER — STAVERTON	EGBJ	GLO	
GUERNSEY	EGJB	GCI	
HAMBLE	EGHM		Closed 1984
HAWARDEN	EGNR	CEG	
HATFIELD	EGTH		
HESTON			Closed 1947
INVERNESS — DALCROSS	EGPE	INV	
IPSWICH	EGSE	IPW	
ISLAY	EGPI	ILY	
JERSEY	EGJJ	JER	
LEEDS/BRADFORD	EGNM	LBA	
LEICESTER — REARSBY			Closed c1964
LIVERPOOL — SPEKE	EGGP	LPL	
LONDON CITY	EGLC	LCY	
LONDON GATWICK	EGKK	LGW	
LONDON HEATHROW	EGLL	LHR	
LONDON STANSTED	EGSS	STN	
LONDON LUTON	EGGW	LTN	
LYDD — FERRYFIELD	EGMD	LYX	
LYMPNE — ASHFORD	EGMK		Closed 1974
MANCHESTER — BARTON	EGCB		
MANCHESTER — RINGWAY	EGCC	MAN	
NEWCASTLE	EGNT	NCL	
NORTHOLT	EGWU		
NORWICH	EGSH	NWI	
NOTTINGHAM — TOLLERTON	EGBN		
OXFORD — KIDLINGTON	EGTK		
PENZANCE HELIPORT — EASTERN GREEN	EGHK	PZE	
PETERBOROUGH — CONINGTON	EGSF		
PETERBOROUGH — SIBSON	EGSP		
PLYMOUTH	EGHD	PLH	
PORTSMOUTH	EGHP		Closed 1973
PRESTWICK	EGPK	PIK	
RADLETT			Closed 1970
REDHILL	EGKR		
RONALDSWAY — ISLE OF MAN	EGNS	IOM	
SHOREHAM	EGKA	ESH	
SOUTHAMPTON — EASTLEIGH	EGHI	SOU	
SOUTHAMPTON MARINE			Closed 1959
SOUTHEND	EGMC	SEN	
SUMBURGH	EGPB	LSI	
SUNDERLAND — USWORTH	EGNU		
TEESSIDE	EGNV	MME	
WHITE WALTHAM	EGLM		
WOODFORD	EGCD		
WYCOMBE AIR PARK — BOOKER	EGTB		
YEOVIL	EGHG		

APPENDIX II.
PASSENGER STATISTICS 1958-1992

London Area Airports

Airport	1958	1963	1968	1973	1978	1983	1988	1992
Heathrow	3,518,832	8,027,445	13,159,019	20,077,270	26,490,960	26,163,800	37,510,200	43,817,000
Gatwick	186,172	966,541	2,059,535	5,728,457	7,759,059	12,471,300	20,744,000	19,670,000
Stansted	20,001	112,095	146,045	172,931	316,744	343,600	1,046,700	1,610,000
Luton		123,892	690,610	3,216,522	2,058,085	1,708,200	2,796,600	1,974,000
Southend	183,230	460,960	488,697	384,842	236,052	90,600	95,400	
London City						Opened Oct 1987	10,600	132,900
Battersea Heliport		413	1,104	8,662	8,742	6,800		

Other Airports

Airport	1958	1963	1968	1973	1978	1983	1988	1992
Aberdeen	32,950	57,040	97,606	259,984	1,200,286	1,747,800	1,612,100	2,126,000
Belfast	286,156	649,676	981,319	1,312,953	1,176,317	1,389,000	2,176,200	2,218,000
Belfast Harbour				Opened for passenger traffic 1983		85,500	400,400	567,000
Benbecula	7,587	16,470	14,189	22,756	23,803	24,900	29,600	
Birmingham	152,996	353,895	557,185	1,131,845	1,305,210	1,559,800	2,786,000	3,537,000
Blackpool	54,285	138,737	149,138	142,571	108,152	77,600	157,900	
Bournemouth	29,411	178,774	35,310	118,764	148,141	127,800	100,700	
Bristol	30,329	78,881	129,668	288,864	232,891	330,800	705,400	920,000
Cambridge			6,365	7,091	23,765	12,400	18,700	
Cardiff	35,179	93,083	130,412	283,550	234,204	383,000	619,400	603,000
Carlisle		Opened 1960					4,600	3,200
Coventry			11,208	8,754	4,388	23,300	11,200	
Dundee		Opened 1963					21,800	8,400
East Midlands		Opened 1965	183,917	515,960	547,591	960,300	1,329,500	1,224,000

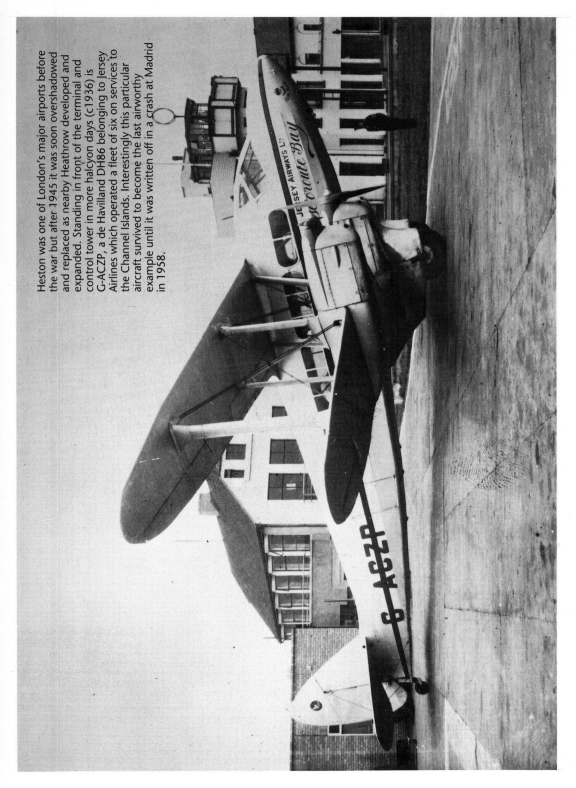

Heston was one of London's major airports before the war but after 1945 it was soon overshadowed and replaced as nearby Heathrow developed and expanded. Standing in front of the terminal and control tower in more halcyon days (c1936) is G-ACZP, a de Havilland DH86 belonging to Jersey Airlines which operated a fleet of six on services to the Channel Islands. Interestingly this particular aircraft survived to become the last airworthy example until it was written off in a crash at Madrid in 1958.

Other Airports – continued

Airport	1958	1963	1968	1973	1978	1983	1988	1992
Edinburgh	111,540	389,821	616,129	877,182	1,137,355	1,275,300	207,380	2,500,000
Exeter				78,881	76,308	87,800	165,400	
Glasgow	426,763	996,264	1,387,210	2,142,437	2,153,322	2,440,500	3,634,400	4,477,000
Gloucester					10,496	17,774	4,900	3,300
Humberside						44,036	72,200	135,300
Inverness	20,246	31,850	50,085	133,695	143,870	173,700	186,500	
Islay	10,778	14,116	15,588	17,950	11,492	11,800	20,200	
Isle of Man	183,811	302,239	378,376	464,482	345,769	268,500	479,800	465,000
Isles of Scilly	25,034	30,071	59,125	73,428	96,432	72,000	103,300	
Kirkwall	21,596	38,628	59,139	75,013	103,232	86,600	95,200	
Leeds/Bradford	27,154	147,025	288,148	280,092	331,548	386,000	683,400	679,000
Liverpool	131,164	294,459	427,472	555,885	287,029	235,100	351,600	462,000
Lydd	222,828	204,277	102,778	1,576	74,522	128,600	2,200	1,796
Manchester	447,171	1,117,774	1,459,773	2,574,214	3,408,206	5,075,900	9,503,900	11,222,000
Newcastle	42,883	184,387	324,411	616,595	759,508	990,900	1,395,200	
Norwich					64,737	165,304	164,700	177,400
Penzance Heliport			Opened 1970	59,125	69,022	91,697	79,200	90,200
Plymouth							90,100	112,100
Prestwick	110,657	196,861	362,006	386,478	362,664	250,000	302,300	
Southampton	86,561	51,574	231,301	308,479	281,741	276,200	456,500	426,000
Stornoway	15,026	29,266	31,839	46,319	54,518	58,900	64,600	
Sumburgh	12,716	16,371	23,493	73,360	n/a	229,700	310,400	390,000
Swansea			2,510	2,352	1,331	1,900	1,200	
Teesside		Opened 1964	72,729	188,895	296,587	304,400	307,300	311,000
Tiree	2,766	3,883	3,900	4,335	3,634	4,200	5,600	
Wick	19,691	23,311	27,912	33,140	32,265	30,000	26,400	

Channel Islands Airports

Airport	1958	1963	1968	1973	1978	1983	1988
Alderney	16,967	23,581	39,971	68,717	69,508	78,000	92,000
Guernsey	159,391	279,041	379,701	488,929	524,604	536,600	825,400
Jersey	486,920	829,325	1,042,497	1,439,412	1,396,660	1,353,700	1,846,400

Note: Figures for 1992 are for the 12 months to July 1992